LEAVING LARGE

The Stories of a Food Addict

LEAVING LARGE
The Stories of a Food Addict

MICHELLE PETTIES

Brand New Now Press
Annapolis, Maryland

LEAVING LARGE

The Stories of a Food Addict

MICHELLE PETTIES

Published by Brand New Now Press

LEAVING LARGE: The Stories of a Food Addict
Copyright © September 2021 by Michelle Petties

ISBN: Hardback: 978-1-7379201-0-6
       Paperback: 978-1-7379201-1-3
       E-book: 978-1-7379201-2-0

Cover Inspiration by Olivia Garrett-Miller

Cover and Layout Design by Jana Rade

Cover Photography by Tommie Adams Photography

Brand New Now Press Books are available at special discounts when purchased in bulk as well as for fundraising or educational use. For details, contact the Publisher by emailing michellep@leavinglarge.com

Printed in the United States of America First Printing September 2021

Dedication

This book is dedicated to:

My mother who gave me life
Sara Jean Petties Perdue

My grandmother who shaped my life
Annie Mae Welch Petties

My aunt who said, "live your life"
Dorothy Victoria Petties Jones

My aunt who saved my life
Josie Ann Elizabeth (Baby Doll) Petties Spears

My sister who said, "write about your life"
Myrna Rene Perdue Marks

Food Stories

"We delight in the beauty of the butterfly, but rarely admit the changes it has gone through to achieve that beauty."

~ MAYA ANGELOU

Foreword

The moment Michelle told me about this book, I was thrilled and excited for her. Of course, I would be. First, because she is one of my own, one of many talented sisters who made a name and place for herself in the early days of Radio One; next, because I have had a front row seat on her journey and have seen and felt her transformation for myself; and finally, because she is now blessed, as I have been, to be living in her divine purpose. Read on and you will understand what I mean.

Once Michelle explained the book's premise, it resonated with me immediately. I was intrigued and frankly, impressed. *Leaving Large* flips the script on an issue that sorely needs flipping. The stories are the heart and soul of this memoir. They are reality. They are raw. They are relatable and familiar— Food Stories. They expose the truth about why and how we eat when we are not hungry. These stories give us the information we need to exercise our personal power over food with an incredible truth that is both brilliant and simple.

Michelle dropped 60 pounds and more importantly, she is not at risk of gaining the weight back. Like many, I know firsthand how difficult it can be to lose even 10 or 20 pounds and how easy it is to use food to fill emotional emptiness. But I never gave much thought to the "why" of it until reading *Leaving Large*. I was anxious to get through all the stories and wrap my head around the narratives. Certain themes kept recurring—unifying, parallel themes. Story. Power. Voice. Reality. Truth. I came to understand the stories were about giving us information to gain power over food and eating and how to ultimately apply the same principles to our lives.

When I arrived in DC so many years ago, I was a divorced, single-minded, single mother committed to making a way in the world for myself and my son, Alfred. First, I was a Howard University lecturer, years later, the first woman to own a radio station ranked #1 in any major market and the first African-American woman to head a publicly traded company. I have been described as, "a poor little (Black) girl from Omaha, Nebraska". Well, I built Urban One by challenging and changing that story—by telling the story of me and my people. In fact, I made it my job to tell the story of the Black community. I am still fiercely devoted to my son, and now grandson, and I am also unwavering in my commitment to the millions of Black people served by Urban One properties, Radio One, TV One, IDigital, CleoTV, One Solution, and Reach Media. These platforms thrive today, in part, because we inform; we inspire; we entertain; and we are guided by one unifying principle—my mantra, for over 40 years—information is power. Having a voice for our own people is the most important thing we do. Upending false narratives — the lies we believe— the ones we tell ourselves and others tell us, rejecting the status quo, introducing new concepts, innovative thoughts, different ideas, assessing situations from a fresh perspective. That's what I have done all my career. And that's exactly what Michelle does in Leaving Large. The parallels and intersections are undeniable. That's why once I started reading it, I couldn't stop.

Michelle shows us that we each have the power within to change our weight by changing our Food Stories. We must be aware that they exist and what they are. The power is in our stories, something I've known since before I left Omaha. I am so honored to present **Leaving Large** because I know this disease, obesity, is having a devastating impact on the Black community. We have all heard that your health is your wealth. The reality is, as I have said information is power, we cannot access our wealth or exercise our power to its fullest without our health. Well, we are being robbed. Yes, her Food Stories shine a bright light on how we all come to a place of eating for the wrong reasons. Through Michelle's stories, I could see how she came to mismanage food. I could also see how it could happen with all of us, me included, for that matter. It is also clear that how we choose to manage food is a metaphor for how we manage our lives as a community. While the vehicle is food, the stories are about life.

Michelle manages to write stories to break this food thing down in a way that's meaningful. I needed this book. I saw myself in the stories. This book is about discovery and eating but it's also about tapping into your personal power. The information in these stories provided insight on how to deal with food in a different way and life in a different way. In **Leaving Large**, Michelle shows us all how to access the information in the stories of our past to change the stories of our future to be healthy and to look and feel fabulous!

So go ahead, read and reread the stories. Apply the lessons and then expect your stories to change.

Cathy Hughes
Founder and Chairperson Urban One, Inc.

Introduction

Thank you so much for purchasing this book, investing in yourself, and joining me on this *Leaving Large* journey. I wrote the Food Stories in this book for myself, but I published them for you. My stories are your stories. Recognizing your own Food Stories is just the first leg of a journey that will transform how you view food and the role it plays in your life. I am committed to raising our collective consciousness around why we eat, what we eat, and sharing my real time insights and experiences about food and eating for the right reasons. To that end, I invite you to join my *Leaving Large* community where you can receive free support, coaching, motivation, and inspiration for your journey.

FOOD STORY 1

Where It All Began

WHERE IT ALL BEGAN

The seeds for the idea of this book were planted at a family cookout on my uncle's farm in the summer of 1996. It all began when I asked my favorite uncle if he wanted some watermelon. I figured he would say yes. After all, the watermelon on deck that day was big, bright red, and juicy; it looked so sweet and refreshing. I couldn't wait to dig into its cool, crisp deliciousness.

"Billy," I said, using the only name I ever called my uncle. "Do you want some of this watermelon?"

"No," he replied.

"Why not?" I asked. "Do you not like watermelon? You're just not hungry? Do you want some later?" Everyone else was enjoying it. But not Billy. I thought it was odd.

"I don't eat watermelon," Billy explained, still uninterested.

"But why not?" I insisted. "You don't like it?"

Realizing that I am not about to let this go, my uncle, who was in his late 70s by then, finally relented. He told me the story that would—years later—forever change my beliefs about food, why we crave it, and why we binge on certain kinds of food.

As it turns out, my uncle's disinterest in watermelon had nothing to do with taste. In fact, as a child he had quite a fondness for watermelon. So much so that when he was a boy of about seven or eight in Marshall, Texas, he, and some friends stole a watermelon from a neighbor's garden. They were just having fun. It was something to do on a hot summer day.

But what was supposed to be fun took a bad turn. When his father, my grandfather, found out about the incident, he was not happy. Well, my grandfather, with arms strengthened from years of pounding nails into railroad ties as a Texas railman, beat my uncle with a belt for all he was worth. There was no way that my grandfather, who served as a church trustee, would let

21

anyone think his son was a thief or that he wasn't providing for his family. Clearly, he administered a whipping that my uncle never forgot.

My uncle had not eaten watermelon since.

I was saddened and deeply shaken by his story. Still, I had another question.

"Well, Billy, that was over seventy years ago," I said. "Now that you look back, do you think maybe the lesson was supposed to be, 'Thou shalt not steal'?"

"I don't eat watermelon," he repeated.

So, I left it at that.

Many years later, I reflected on this story, and it hit me: My uncle's experience with watermelon was so traumatic that even after seven decades, he still could not bring himself to eat it. The memories associated with this food that he once loved as a boy were just too painful, which he would risk reliving if he ate the fruit.

This led me to ask other questions: Could the opposite be true? That is, is it possible that our cravings and binges are rooted in certain memories and experiences that are so pleasurable that they drive us to eat certain foods? Is it also possible that, like my uncle who had stopped eating watermelon because of a bad experience, we crave certain foods because they evoke good memories?

The answers to these questions led me to what I call Food Identity, which I define as the way we think, feel, act, and move around food. Our Food Identities are born out of our Food Stories, the events, experiences, and memories that form our beliefs, attitudes, and habits about food, eating, and hunger. Navigating through my own Food Stories helped me to develop an individualized process to finally manage cravings, bingeing, and overeating.

Throughout my journey I figured out how to find, face, and rewrite my toxic Food Stories and replace them with brand new Food Stories. Changing my Food Stories empowered me to change my Food Identity. When I changed what food means in my life and separated my food interactions and experiences from the feelings they evoked, the scale started moving downward. This put me on a path toward wholeness and well-being, and I began to experience freedom from food addiction for the first time in my life. I'm sure you want the scale to move in the right direction for you too.

Leaving Large is a collection of personal Food Stories, learnings, and lessons that transformed my mind and body. I share Food Stories that kept me trapped, and ultimately released me from a 42-year cycle of obesity and yo-yo dieting. My journey, through these Food Stories, allowed me to discover the peace, pride, confidence, freedom, power, and joy hidden beneath four decades and 700 pounds of fat. (That is how much weight I lost and gained over the years, a pattern I repeated over and over.)

We all have Food Stories. That is, my Food Stories are not about me. They are about you. They are about us. We all have Food Stories to tell. We, however, seldom recognize them for what they are, focus on how they came to be, or how they control us. Consequently, we go through life mindlessly eating excessively large portions of this and that, whether it is crab legs or chicken wings, potato salad or apple pie, because our yet-to-be-unpacked Food Stories are dictating how we think, feel, act, and move around food.

I can promise you this: after you read even a few stories in this book, you will never look at the food you eat, and the food you think you love, the same. You will see that much of what you eat is an attempt to recreate an experience, and that continually trying to relive an experience through food may not necessarily be in the best interests of your health and wellbeing. In fact, it might be killing you.

All this time, I bet you thought you were "living large." Well, now the time has come to begin "leaving large." Let's get going!

It's Not About the Food

It's About the Story Behind the Food

And I Would Love to Learn More About Your Food Story

FOOD STORY #1: WHERE IT ALL BEGAN

This story illustrates what happens when the lure of enjoying a favorite food with friends leads to unintended and unexpected consequences. My uncle decided early on that the price of eating watermelon again was too high.

"The memories associated with this food that he once loved as a boy were just too painful, which he would risk reliving if he ate the fruit."

Does this Food Story bring up any painful food memories for you?

You can share your Food Story with me here:
michellep@leavinglarge.com

FOOD STORY 2

Pizzagate Breakdown

PIZZAGATE BREAKDOWN

The book you are reading was really supposed to be a cookbook. It's what my doctor suggested I write after losing 60 pounds, while following her guidance. However, as I sat down to write, my thoughts kept going back to the day I scarfed down five giant slices of veggie pizza in about ten minutes.

I knew something was seriously wrong when I did that.

I have always dressed to impress, no matter what size I was. In 2018, when I was attending a professional conference in Crystal City, Virginia, I was 215 pounds, a size 18 squeezing into a size 16, just a few pizza slices away from not even being able to do that. Up until that day, I thought I had this overeating thing under control. But pizza, a food I have loved since college, had something else in mind. As I found myself eating slice after slice, I knew I had to do something different from what I had tried up to this point.

I sensed this was not purely about lack of willpower, self-control, or discipline. Something else was going on that had me on a hamster wheel of dieting. And I was tired. I was ready to get off. "Please God, help me!"

After the pizza breakdown, the first thing I thought to do was go to the wellness doctor I had been seeing regularly. She had mentioned her weight-loss programs during previous visits. Now it was time to take her up on her offer.

I was in such a panic that I didn't even bother to make an appointment. Fortunately, when I showed up, my doctor didn't have any other patients to see. She saw my distress and kindly agreed to take me right away. But what she said next was a shock.

"It's your job," my doctor said matter-of-factly. "Your job is making you fat. Your job is having an adverse effect on your health."

I could not believe she was attacking my career. Ever since I graduated from college in 1981, my career has served as a constant and reliable source of pleasure and income. Now I was being barraged with questions.

How many hours a week do you work? What is your commute like? When did you start wearing Depends? How long has your weight been a problem? What is the most you have ever weighed? When was that? Does obesity run in your family? How about heart disease? How long have you had memory problems? Do you exercise? Do you have diabetes or high blood pressure? Are you menopausal? Are your hormones out of balance?

She took all the information I provided and concluded that I was suffering from stress—and it was potentially fatal.

"People die from stress," my doctor said with empathy in her voice. "It's your job."

As empathetic as she was about my plight, I could not wrap my head around what she was saying. How could the career that I worked so hard to build and loved so much be stressful? At the same time, the fact that I had my pizza breakdown on the job suggested that my doctor might be onto something.

The prior three days I had been attending an intense but enjoyable professional development conference for people who work in public television sales. I had been networking and exchanging ideas with other aspiring and high achieving public television professionals from all over the country. It was interesting and informative. I felt capable and accomplished. I had every reason to feel like I was on top of the world.

I landed the position at Maryland Public Television in 2017, one that was tailor-made for me. Aside from my constant weight struggles, I saw myself as the picture of professional success. But looking back on that conference now, I know my weight was, well, weighing on me.

All throughout the conference, my colleagues from around the country were networking, socializing, meeting for happy hour after the sessions, revisiting the day's discussions and deepening their personal and professional connections—the kind of connections you make when you share a bucket of chicken wings and a cold craft beer or a glass of wine. Since I lived in the vicinity, I didn't book a hotel room. At the end of each day, I returned to my home and missed the camaraderie that these types of conferences offer. It left me feeling disconnected, out of place, different. And the fact that I was slowly gaining back weight that I had lost didn't help.

On the final day of the conference, it had all gotten to me. Despite my professional success, my personal success—at least in terms of losing weight—just could not match it. I was now sitting in my doctor's office, a personal failure. You might as well have called me a "D" student: disgusted, disappointed, desperate, and distraught over these demons I thought I had defeated. And now I was diagnosed with career-related stress?

The doctor must have been right, though. Bingeing on pizza alone at home is one thing. Doing it at a professional conference in front of your colleagues is quite another.

My unhealthy love affair with pizza goes back to my days in college and the early years of my career when pizza served as my go-to food for comfort. I used pizza to celebrate and reward success. I only stopped feasting on pizza when I started following low carb, high protein diets.

That's why the pizza breakdown at the conference caught me by surprise. I hadn't binged on pizza in at least five years. Why did I lose control on this day?

Sitting in my doctor's office searching for answers, I was miserable. I didn't feel like I needed another diet, but I felt compelled to give it another shot. I felt I owed it to myself to try her program.

Over the years, I have spent thousands and thousands of dollars on countless diet doctors, diet plans, diet programs, diet pills, diet videos, diet cookies, diet groups, psychotherapy, and multiple surgeries—all to get a body I could love. Cabbage soup, low carb, no carb, low-fat, no-fat, protein bars, cookies, powders, and shakes, I have tried 'em all!

My doctor wouldn't let up on the questions, one right after the other in rapid succession. Do you take vitamins? How many hours a night do you sleep? How much water do you drink? How much alcohol do you consume? How often do you eat out? What do you eat for lunch? For breakfast? For dinner? They were just questions, but they felt like accusations. I loved my job and felt lucky to have had a nearly 40-year career that I was born for.

What on earth was she going on about? What did that mean? It was crazy and unbelievable. Soon, I couldn't hear what she was saying. My job was stressful? Hell, all these damn questions were stressful. I needed a break. I needed relief...and soon I got it. I saw my doctor's lips moving, but soon I only heard the calming voice of my grandmother, "Here, Michelle, add up the totals for these orders."

I loved math and was helping my grandmother, who had been a full-time homemaker while raising my mother and her siblings, with her new side hustle: selling Avon. It was the 1960s. She was in her mid-50s, determinedly carving out her independence, learning how to drive, getting a car, and becoming one of two Black Avon representatives in Marshall, Texas.

Part of me suspects that as much as my grandmother did these things for herself, she also did them to set an example for me and her then-grown children. We would both get dressed in our best, then I would accompany her on her sales calls and quietly observe as she made her presentations. I saw how much her clients enjoyed her visits and the products she delivered. I have no doubt that these early experiences influenced my decision to embark upon a career in sales. A former student of the famous Wiley College, my grandmother placed a high value on education. She longed to be a teacher but dropped out after marrying my grandfather. She held firmly to the belief that we are all products of our habits and "what you do at home, you will do in public. Someone is always watching you." She loved to travel. We frequently jumped on the train to visit her friends in other cities, taking full advantage of my grandfather's travel benefits as a Texas and Pacific Railway employee. Decades before Oprah and The Secret—the critically acclaimed self-help movie and book that teaches people how to change their life by changing their thoughts—my grandmother preached to me about the importance of heartfelt gratitude and the power of a simple handwritten thank you note. Her financial philosophy was, "Save before you spend; live below your means; don't give your money away on interest; and layaway is disrespectful to Black people."

I looked forward to helping my grandmother bag up her orders every week and calculate her profits. Her trust filled me with great pride and pleasure. The little cosmetic samples she sent my way were rewards for my able assistance. Let's get back to my doctor's office. Something inexplicable happened to me that day. As I readied my arm for what would become daily hormone injections that I would eventually give myself, and listened as my doctor reviewed the protocols, I vowed that this time would be different. My journey back in time, where I let my grandmother's spirit speak, gave rise to a few of my own questions: Why am I here again? Why can't I get my body and habits in line with my heart? Why can't I control my weight? Why haven't I gotten a handle on this? Why? Why? Why? What haven't I learned? What am I missing?

I struggled with my weight all my adult life, constantly yo-yoing up and down. For years, I would focus on changing what I was eating without changing what I was feeling and thinking, or more importantly, considering the origin of those thoughts and feelings. This dawning realization soon gave way to new insight, intuition, and understanding about food, eating, and hunger. Questions that were once a source of frustration and confusion landed differently and ignited this superpower of clarity and vision. Sure, I understood that obesity posed a threat to my longevity and quality of life. But it was only when my livelihood was threatened did my superpower kick in and allow true transformation to begin. That was the day I started to slay the pizza demon, its cohorts, and tag-alongs, once and for all! I haven't had pizza since or any desire for it. And to think, there was a point when pizza meant so much to me. But not anymore.

It's Not About the Food

It's About the Story Behind the Food

And I Would Love to Learn More About Your Food Story

FOOD STORY #2: PIZZAGATE BREAKDOWN

In this story, a pizza meltdown at a business conference led to a mind shifting breakthrough for me.

"I sensed this was not purely about lack of willpower, self-control, or
discipline. Something else was going on that had me on a hamster wheel
of dieting. And I was tired. I was ready to get off. "Please God, help me!""

Can you think of a time when it felt as if you didn't
have control over how much you were eating?

Please share your Food Story with me here: michellep@leavinglarge.com

FOOD STORY 3

Lunchroom Misery

LUNCHROOM MISERY

U sually when you see images of the first Black children to integrate America's public schools in the 1950s and 60s, they show the Black kids being escorted by Federal Agents or U.S. soldiers to all-White schools as angry White mobs protest their presence. That's what happened with the "Little Rock Nine" when they became the first Black students to attend Little Rock Central High School in 1957, the year before I was born. And it happened to Ruby Bridges when she became the first Black girl to attend William Frantz Elementary School in New Orleans in 1960.

Norman Rockwell captured Ruby's historic walk to school in a famous 1964 painting titled "The Problem We All Live With." In the painting, a then-six-year-old Ruby is seen carrying her school supplies while being accompanied by four uniformed U.S. Marshals. Scrawled on a wall behind Ruby was the word "NIGGER" and the initials "KKK." Traces of a tomato that someone had thrown at little Ruby were splattered against the wall.

If Norman Rockwell had visited my school, Sam Houston Elementary, when I became one of the first Black students to integrate it in September of 1965, he would have had a vastly different picture to paint.

The Struggle for Acceptance

If Rockwell had captured me during my first days as a second grader at Sam Houston Elementary, the painting would not have shown a little Black girl flanked by four U.S. Marshals being taunted by an angry White mob. Instead, it would have shown a lonely Black girl sitting at the lunch table all by herself. No one threw food at me like they threw at Ruby. The only food in my picture would have been my sandwiches: bologna and cheese, tuna or chicken salad, peanut butter and jelly, pressed ham, and cheese. Sweet treats like Hostess CupCakes, Twinkies, and Sno Balls often completed the menu. Food dulled the pain of isolation and helped me cope with the stress of those first lonely lunches as I struggled for acceptance.

I really missed my friends at Paul Laurence Dunbar, the Black elementary school about a mile from our house. I watched longingly through the window as the neighborhood kids passed my house on Travis Street, on their way to Dunbar.

The difference between Paul Laurence Dunbar and Sam Houston Elementary school was like night and day. Whereas Sam Houston had manicured grounds enclosed by a beautiful chain link fence, Dunbar sat on a ditch-encircled hill. When it rained, that ditch would fill and overflow with rushing water. I was afraid to jump over the gushing water and my grandmother would have to get out of the car in the rain to coax or lift me over what to me at the time looked like treacherous waters. In fact, my grandparents transferred me to Sam Houston because my grandmother had grown tired of this drill. That's when she became an activist and jumped on the Brown vs. Board of Education bandwagon and enrolled me in Sam Houston, which was also much closer to our house.

My new school was physically closer, but my friends at Dunbar were still closer to my heart.

Missing My Friends

I missed Amelia—hands down the smartest person in our class. Her mother, Miss Dorothy, made sure of that. Charlotte and I shared the same middle name, and our mothers grew up together. Rene's house on Johnson Street was one of the few places my grandmother would drop me off to play all day. Barbara always brought the best lunches, certainly the ones with the best desserts. Sheila thought I wanted her boyfriend, but I didn't care nothing 'bout no Denny Cooper. Besides, my little six-year-old heart was set on Jesse Fisher. Sheila's big mama made the best lemon pies in the city. Kathy Diane Jackson, may she rest in peace, always took my lunch. And Esther Davis, my cousin Pettis, had a big-time crush on her. Now I only saw these people, my friends, on Sundays at Galilee Baptist Church.

As I made my way to what would become my school home for the next five years, I knew my friends at Dunbar would be involved in first-day-of-school-rituals for students attending Black schools, getting locker assignments and brown paper book covers, and sandpaper to clean the hand-me-down textbooks from the White schools. At Sam Houston, I had no idea what I would be doing, or more importantly, who I would be eating lunch with.

The White kids at Sam Houston weren't mean to me. They just didn't know me. I didn't know them, and they weren't in a rush to get to know me. So, lunch was a difficult time, especially since I was such a social person back then. But my grandmother always made sure I had plenty to eat. She even reluctantly made BLT for me after I saw one of my White classmates with one and wanted the same thing, my attempt to fit in. No longer content with a brown bag, I begged for a lunch box with a thermos. I eventually got it, too.

Finding My Place

After several weeks, I became more comfortable and made a place for myself at Sam Houston. I took to heart my grandmother's simple advice to "do your best." Over the years, I grew to love my time at the school, as well as my teachers and classmates. Still, it wasn't exactly a piece of cake.

I was the biggest kid in my class, but I felt like I had to fight for visibility. And sometimes I suspected that my size and color were getting in the way of things I wanted. I remember when our music teacher, Mrs. Shaw, announced that our class would perform the "12 Days of Christmas" for the upcoming holiday program and that everyone would have a part. I was excited at first, but my delight soon turned to disappointment when I learned that I had been selected to be one of the five golden rings. Not that golden rings aren't precious and cool, but I wanted to be one of the beautiful, graceful swans and wear the pretty petticoats. The swans were clearly the stars of the production. After class, I approached Mrs. Shaw and told her I wanted to be a swan. If she was surprised by the boldness of my request, she didn't show it and was rather matter of fact in her refusal. While she didn't say it directly, I got the message: "You're too big and too dark to be a swan." I guess I should have been happy I wasn't the partridge in the pear tree.

As trying as it was being one of a few Black kids in Ms. Eubanks' second grade class, and one of a handful in the entire school, it presaged the various social situations in which I would later find myself in college and in my career, as the only person of color, or one of a few, in the room.

Workplace Parallels

That's how it was when I accepted an entry-level position at the advertising giant, J. Walter Thompson, as an assistant to Donna Wald, one of the most powerful women in the Dallas media market. It was the end of June 1981, and after five years, I had finally received my B.A. in Radio and Television from the University of Texas at Arlington. I would be earning $10,800 a year, which was decent money at the time. I felt lucky and grateful to have landed such a coveted position. While I was in college, I heard repeatedly that it was tough to get a job in advertising, and even tougher for Black folks to break into this competitive and overwhelmingly White field. In a way, it was true.

I sensed how difficult it was to break into the business when interviewing for a position with Blair Radio. I researched Blair Radio prior to the interview, and I let them know it. Blair was a top tier organization. I was nervous, but confident and delighted that I didn't have to take a typing test. A few days later, sales manager Randell Harris called and said they offered the job to someone else. I was crushed. He quickly halted my disappointment, assuring me with his next words, "Don't be upset. We like you. And we called around to see who else was hiring. Call Donna Wald, now. She is looking for an assistant. Here is the number. She's expecting to hear from you." In an industry known to be cutthroat, this simple, selfless, and unexpected kindness changed the trajectory of my career and life.

My first day at work, I was 30-minutes early, ready to get every available worm. I was excited and intrigued as I entered 13700 Park Central. I had no idea what was waiting behind door #300. I thought I kind of knew, but I really didn't.

I was happy and pleasantly surprised to see two other sistahs in the mix. I was in, but like those early days at Sam Houston Elementary, I still didn't fit in. I was once again the biggest one in the room, but this time it was the conference room instead of the classroom and the lunchroom. It was like elementary school all over again.

During my first country club lunch, I heard the term "expense account." Who knew? When I first saw a bagel, I said something like, "Look at those giant donuts!" Talk about embarrassment. I might as well have worn a button that said, "Hi, I'm a country bumpkin." Nor did I know what to drink at happy hour. Or what makes chicken salad gourmet. Or what to wear for a network premier party.

Soon after attending my first premier party, I figured out why I was passed over for other positions. The room was filled with Amys, Beckys, and Mollys with Farrah Fawcett hair and Bally Fitness bodies. While I was smart and personable, I could not check any of those boxes—big blonde hair and beach body—just as in those early days at Sam Houston. My grandmother's sage advice, my best effort, attitude, and hard work—I soon learned were only getting me so far. As I struggled to fit in, I turned to food for comfort, just as I had during those early lonely days in the cafeteria at Sam Houston.

A Constant Companion

That pattern would repeat itself throughout my career in advertising, as I endeavored to live the financially secure life my grandmother envisioned for me. I loved my job and realized I was blessed and privileged to contribute in a way that was meaningful, interesting and a ton of fun.

But even as I rode the wave of success in my professional life, no matter the time, circumstance, situation or event, food remained my constant companion in the stressful world of advertising sales. This went on for more than 40 years as I freely moved in and out of broadcast organizations — from Dallas to Washington to Atlanta, and back to Washington. My career in advertising and sales included decades of work for major media outlets like

ABC, Disney, and Radio One. I negotiated client campaigns for household brands like McDonald's, T-Mobile, and Coca-Cola.

Entertaining clients at restaurants and venues citywide became my life. As the cycle of eating continued, I eventually ended up in a situation where food threatened not only my life but my very livelihood. The two, you see—food and work—became so intertwined that I used the former to help me cope with the stress of the latter. Until one day, it all came to a head.

It's Not About the Food

It's About the Story Behind the Food

And I Would Love to Learn More About Your Food Story

FOOD STORY #3: LUNCHROOM MISERY

This story shows how the unconscious habit of using food to mask discomfort followed me from childhood well into adulthood.

"While she didn't say it directly, I got the message: "You're too big and too dark to be a swan." I guess I should have been happy I wasn't the partridge in the pear tree."

Can you think of times when you ate for the pleasure of the moment?

Share your Food Story with me here: michellep@leavinglarge.com

FOOD STORY 4

Big Boned and Blue

BIG BONED AND BLUE

When students get weighed, it's supposed to be done in private to spare the children any sort of potential embarrassment. That's according to the Centers for Disease Control, which provides guidelines to states on how schools should collect student weight data as part of its Healthy Schools Initiative.

"Height and weight measurements must not be conducted within sight or hearing distance of other students," the CDC states on its website. "The trained staff member conducting the measurement can-be the only person to see the results and cannot announce them out loud."

I sure wish they had guidelines like this back when I was a sixth grader at Sam Houston Elementary School. Had they, I would have been spared one of the most embarrassing experiences of my life.

Weight Class

It all began during our routine end-of-the-year weight check. This one took place in May of 1970. Not only were we instructed to stand in line to wait our turn at the scale, but the teacher would say our weight out loud as she recorded it in a logbook.

This was never a big deal for me in the past. But this particular year I was in for a surprise. I waited in line for my turn at the scale just like I had done years before – completely oblivious to the humiliation I was about to experience.

I stepped on the scale and looked straight ahead like the teacher told me to. I waited for my teacher's reading of the results. Her words landed like a loud thud. "Michelle Petties, 135 pounds," the teacher said matter-of-factly in front of the entire class.

Those two things–my name and my weight – spoken together in front of my classmates were devastating. It's not that I hadn't been through this before. This particular year I happened to weigh more than anyone in the class, even more than any of the boys.

I felt a sudden rush of embarrassment and self-consciousness. There was never any hiding my size. But to get a clear and scientific confirmation by way of a public announcement that–yes, I was the biggest kid in class, was mortifying.

There was a time when this annual weigh-in was an unremarkable practice, but then something changed–dramatically–on this particular day. For the first time that number – my weight – meant something and it rattled my pre-teen mind.

In Search of Solace

As one of a handful of Black students in an otherwise all-White class, I didn't know at the time – and not sure it would have mattered if I did – that Black girls tend to develop faster than White girls; and food, especially food without a lot of activity, is often the culprit.

After school was dismissed, I rushed home distraught, anxious, and upset seeking solace from the one person in my world who always made everything right.

"Oh, Kitten," my grandmother said, using her pet name for me. "You're not fat. You have big bones."

This time, however, my grandmother's words offered zero comfort. In my distress, I knew the cold, hard, sobering truth. I was: Stout. Chubby. Chunky. Solid. Thick. A Big Girl. I had heard my grandmother and others use these words when talking about me.

These words weren't meant to be hurtful. The matronly ladies at Galilee Baptist Church would flash big, encouraging smiles of admiration along with a remark like, "Ooh, chile! She sure is a healthy one," when describing me. My grandmother would beam with pride at the compliment. That fact that I was so "healthy", a testament that she and my grandfather were doing a fine job keeping me well-fed and taken care of, a weighty responsibility which they took to heart.

On that day in May, a few weeks before my twelfth birthday, I felt for the first time the soul-piercing pain of what it meant to be uncomfortable in my own skin. "Fat and happy" would never be my truth. I had enough of shopping for dresses in the "stout girls" department and wearing girdles and grown folks' hand-me-downs. Something had to change.

Refusing Food

And change I did. It was more than my passing from elementary to junior high school; I was also experiencing a growing sense of self-awareness and self-determination. The summer between sixth and seventh grades, I just wanted to be an average weight and normal size. I didn't want to stand out because of my body. I didn't know, however, that summer would mark the beginning of a 40-year battle for control over my body. I started weighing myself every day–sometimes two or three times a day. I drowned hunger pains with glass after glass of water, and I spent an entire summer battling with my grandmother over food. I would skip meals or only eat exceedingly small amounts, claiming I wasn't hungry or that I had already eaten.

In the past, cleaning my plate had never been an issue for me because I had always been such a people-pleaser. I loved the big smiles, approval, and joy that being a "good eater" brought to the faces of my grandparents. Their joy was born out of the knowledge that food was key to life, which provided every opportunity to live and thrive. And since I was "a seven-month baby", when they took me in, they became vigorously committed to providing for me. I was frequently reminded that food costs money and wasting food that someone had worked hard to buy, prepare, and put on the table was not acceptable. Sticking to my I'm-not-eating plan was especially tricky because the same sweet and loving grandmother–who once shoved me into girdles, instructed me to "eat with my eyes," and denied me a hula hoop because I was too big–was constantly trying to get me to eat more.

Daily, I refused big delicious, down-home, Southern soul food. I also stepped up my physical activity. My workout included jumping rope and jogging. Much to my surprise, my grandmother would help me by counting my jumping jacks and holding my feet down while I did sit-ups. I copied some of the chair routines that Jack LaLanne–known as "The Godfather of Modern Fitness"–did on his TV program. But I was careful to use the kitchen chairs and not the "good" dining room chairs, which ensured that I stayed on my grandmother's good side.

Anyone on the outside looking in might think I possessed unbelievable willpower, rock solid self-control, and unyielding determination. It was something else. I was haunted by my teacher's announcement of my weight in class. Michelle Petties, 135 pounds. Michelle Petties, 135 pounds. Michelle Petties, 135 pounds. Those words reverberated inside my head, sending me on a single-minded mission to escape and erase them.

Trim and Slim

The next semester, September of 1970–the first year of forced integration for the Marshall Independent School District–I found myself on the campus of H. B. Pemberton Junior High School, which became Price T. Young in 1975.

Our first day as newly minted middle schoolers, we all wandered the halls in search of our respective homerooms. Girls stepped out in freshly pressed dresses. Boys squirmed in crisp shirts and stiff jeans. Me? I was ready. I was greased down with Vaseline, brand new, brown, patent leather, penny loafers on my feet, hair freshly pressed and curled, and sporting my first day-of-school ensemble. Finally, after a five-year separation, I would be reunited with my Dunbar classmates. And, for the first time in over five years, I stepped through the doors of my new school confident now that I was no longer the biggest one in my class. I was 122 pounds, after successfully shedding 13 pounds.

Looking back, I'm glad that my school was required to keep tabs on our weight, since we can't fix that which we never face. And whether it's faced publicly or privately, obesity in children, as well as adults, must be faced. If it weren't for that sixth-grade weigh-in, it's likely that I would have continued to pack on the pounds into early adulthood.

At the same time, we, that is teachers, parents, and guardians, can help children proactively stay at a healthy weight, but do it with sensitivity. When it comes to diet, nutrition, and exercise, we shouldn't expect our youth to come up with answers on their own–and potentially the wrong answers after they've been fat-shamed in front of their classmates and peers.

I successfully dumped the extra weight and maintained a healthy weight through middle and high school. I even made the cheerleading squad. Years later I discovered – much to my surprise and contrary to what my grandmother told me–that I don't have big bones after all.

It's Not About the Food

It's About the Story Behind the Food

And I Would Love to Learn More About Your Food Story

FOOD STORY #4: BIG BONED AND BLUE

It wasn't called fat shaming back then. But I was deeply ashamed and embarrassed and took matters into my own hands.

""Oh, Kitten," my grandmother said, using her pet name for me. "You're not fat. You have big bones." This time, however, my grandmother's words offered zero comfort. In my distress, I knew the cold, hard, sobering truth. I was: Stout. Chubby. Chunky. Solid. Thick. A Big Girl."

What would happen if you faced the truth about your body?

I would love for you to share your Food Story
with me: michellep@leavinglarge.com

FOOD STORY 5

Taste of Freedom

TASTE OF FREEDOM

You couldn't really tell me much after I got my first job at the Holiday Inn Restaurant in Marshall, Texas, the summer after I finished high school. Although my grandfather sure did try. It wasn't that he didn't want his granddaughter—the same one he had cherished, cared for and raised since she entered this world as a premature baby—to be a waitress. It wasn't necessarily about the long hours on my feet or male patrons being rude or inappropriate. My grandfather just didn't want his precious grandbaby to work, period. My grandfather was Old School with a capital "O." He believed in taking care of his family, especially the women. "You don't have to work," he would tell me as I ironed my green uniform and polished my white shoes. "I will buy you whatever you need. You just concentrate on your studyin'."

I wasn't tryin' to hear a thing he was tryin' to say. As far as I was concerned, this hotel waitress job represented freedom and independence, a welcome break from the loving yet controlled and sheltered world created by Pete and Pigeon Petties, which is what friends and family called my grandparents. While my friends spent the summer partying and having fun, I was making my own way, working to save money for my freshman year in college.

This job was a triumph.

So much was going on. It was the end of May 1976 and I had just turned eighteen. Voter registration card in one hand (Yes, I planned to vote a certain peanut farmer from Georgia into the White House), Marshall Senior High School diploma in the other. I graduated in the top 5% of my class, thank you very much.

Through Upward Bound—a federal program meant to provide academic support to students who are either poor or who will be the first in their family to go to college—I was attending summer school at Wiley College and racking up college credits before heading off to the University of Texas in Arlington in August. My federal student financial aid had been approved. I had my dorm assignment. On top of that, now I have my very first real job! I was beaming with pride. This was going to be the best summer ever. I was free, Black and eighteen, and I knew just enough to be a danger to myself and others.

It was also a bicentennial year for America. Like much of the nation, I had plenty to celebrate. You see, the Holiday Inn on Interstate 20 in Marshall, Texas, wasn't just any old hotel. It was one of the few establishments in Marshall that had what was considered fine dining; the other two were Gables Restaurant and the Marshall Country Club. I had only been in a fine dining restaurant once, that was at Disneyland in 1969. Now, I was about to be working at one, making my own money.

I knew this all upset my grandfather, who probably blamed my independent streak on my grandmother—with her Avon-selling, car-driving self. But the way I saw it, he only had to tolerate it for a few more months before I headed off to college and started living my own life.

A New World

When I walked through the swinging doors of the kitchen at that Holiday Inn, it opened me up to a whole new world of culinary delights. My first night on the job, Billy Ray, the evening grill man, showed me the ropes. "Bring water to the table and get the drink order." Got it. "Serve the salads first, on cold salad plates." Why are plates cold? "Remember the bread baskets and butter." Oh! "Steaks are served well-done, medium, medium-well, medium-rare and rare." Huh? "Baked potatoes come with butter, sour cream, cheese, and chives." I had never even heard of a chive. "You don't have to write out the whole word; just abbreviate. Your tickets don't always come up in order." Okay. "That money on the table; that's your tip." Tip? What's that? There was a lot to learn, and it all seemed so foreign.

While waitressing at a fine dining establishment was a little more complicated and lucrative than I imagined, it also came with another perk: free food. Billy Ray explained that each shift, we could order whatever we wanted on the menu, except steak. The menu was filled with plenty of mouth-watering food, some of which I had never heard of: Grilled Rueben. Chef's Salad with Chunky Blue Cheese Dressing. Chicken Fried Steak. French Dip. Club Sandwich. I was curious about all of it, but my eyes settled on the Monte Cristo.

My first bite was so exquisite that I laughed out loud because it was so good! For the uninitiated, a Monte Cristo is a deep fried, egg-dipped ham and cheese sandwich sprinkled with powdered sugar, a menu staple during the 70s and 80s. I still remember the golden-brown triangles regally assembled in the middle of the plate and surrounded by crispy hot fries and sprinkles of powdered sugar that speckled the edges of the plate. I had never experienced anything like it. And in one bite, food once again became a source of joy, entertainment, and adventure. It didn't take long to abandon the fresh vegetables my grandmother served at home; I was always working and eating on the job, something I would end up doing throughout my career in advertising sales, which would ultimately lead to a lifelong battle against overeating.

At the time, this new food just represented a certain type of freedom. Little did I know that my newfound freedom would become the gateway to a certain form of bondage.

Size Increases

The first bite of something refreshingly different, but oh so good, affected my taste buds in a way that I could never have imagined. As my taste buds were being reprogrammed, they began dictating the choices I made about food rather than my rational mind directing me to what I knew was better for me. Everything I was taught about food was being thrown to the wind, and that's where it stayed. I paid a hefty price for that, too.

When I first started working, right before America's 200th birthday and the summer between high school and college, my waitress uniform was a size 10. Just a few months later, when I left for college, I was wearing a size 14. Fortunately, the uniforms were supplied.

There's this phrase called the "Freshman 15," which refers to the 15 pounds that college students, particularly women, are said to gain during their freshman year. Well, I'm here to tell you that Michelle Petties—ever the high-achiever—managed to gain her Freshman 15 before she even set foot on a college campus.

By the end of my sophomore year that fifteen had turned to fifty. I guess I could heap some of the blame on the cafeteria ladies at Lipscomb Hall, my dorm at UT Arlington. They were so supportive and loveable, and in their own way they looked out for the few Black UTA students. They were proud of the Black students attending such a big majority-serving university; they showed their pride and support by putting a little extra on our plate. They would often say things like, "Well, baby, you make sure you study hard." Followed by, "Let me give you a little extra chili." Couple that with lots of restaurant eating and you have a recipe for obesity.

More Free Food

As if it weren't bad enough that I worked as a waitress and put on weight before college, I also spent my last two years of college—and a year or so after—working as a waitress and putting on even more weight. This time I was a waitress at Coco's, an extremely popular West Coast family-style restaurant similar to Denny's. Just like the Holiday Inn, the workers got a free meal on every shift. Since I often worked double shifts, that meant I often got double the food.

It was at Coco's during the late 1970s that I experienced my first of many gourmet burgers—the ones stacked high with fixings such as avocados, grilled mushrooms, blue cheese, and other exotic cheeses. Well, a gourmet burger meal was not complete without decadent desserts. Suddenly, pecan pie, strawberry shortcake, and other great desserts became my new norm. It was easy for me to rationalize eating so much free food. I felt like I had worked for it, like they owed it to me. That's right; I felt entitled.

Food eventually became more about the restaurant experience, one that I could easily access, and less about eating right, like I did back home.

I didn't cook at home. I just ate at the restaurant because the food was free. There were other kinds of food on the menu, but I had gotten into the habit of eating burgers and fries, so I didn't pay for the other options — healthy or not — any mind.

Even after I stopped working in restaurants, I was still fascinated by the dining out experience. This undisciplined, unrestrained hunger for new experiences was not without consequences. This habit continued even after I finished college and started my career in advertising sales. My criteria: What's the tastiest? The winners were always greasy and sweet. Little did I realize then that these habits would curse and cripple my body, well-being, and self-esteem for the next four decades of my life. It may have started with an early jump on the Freshman 15, however, it led to the gain and loss of hundreds of pounds for many years. Until one day, fed up, I went to my doctor. I was desperate to halt the constant accumulation of weight once and for all.

It's Not About the Food

It's About the Story Behind the Food

And I Would Love to Learn More About Your Food Story

FOOD STORY #5: TASTE OF FREEDOM

Proof that freedom and bondage are two sides of the same coin.

"There's this phrase called the "Freshman 15," which refers to the 15 pounds that college students, particularly women, are said to gain during their freshman year. Well, I'm here to tell you that Michelle Petties—ever the high-achiever—managed to gain her Freshman 15 before she even set foot on a college campus."

Do you treat food as a means to an end or the end itself?

Please take a few moments to share your Food Story
with me: michellep@leavinglarge.com

FOOD STORY 6

Fresh off the Farm

FRESH OFF THE FARM

When the recession of 2008 hit, my life of plenty took a turn. Suddenly, I went from driving a Mercedes to walking to the Metro. I could no longer afford nights on the town dining on blackened and stuffed salmon with Cajun cream sauce. The times dictated that I ask myself, "How many different vegetables am I able to mix with this canned salmon to make it last all week?" That one question was transformational. That one question saved me during this period because simply put, I couldn't afford mass quantities of food, fancy or otherwise. The plain, unadorned vegetables I used to ignore or dismiss became crucial for survival.

My financial collapse forced me back to the basics, to a simpler time. Growing up with grandparents who owned a farm meant fresh, garden vegetables were rarely missing from the dinner table. More evenings than I can remember, at sunset, my grandparents and I would pile into their old but reliable green truck and head north on Highway 59 to tend our small farm on Fern Lake Road, just outside the city limits of Marshall.

My grandfather retired after more than twenty-five years as a laborer, and later as a foreman for the old Texas and Pacific Railway. He immediately went to work on the farm. In a short number of years, he almost single-handedly transformed three acres of wild blackberry patches, a few plum and peach trees, and a little wandering stream into a worthwhile enterprise. Even now, I don't believe I fully appreciate the magnitude of his efforts.

Our farm had a chicken coop complete with baby chicks, a barnyard rooster, chickens that would lay fresh brown eggs, and some that could be turned into savory stewed chicken and buttermilk dumplings. There were a few horses, a lot of free-ranging cows, and a Brahman bull occasionally sent out to stud. We had a pen filled with dozens of premium hogs, which, by the way, are much meaner, nastier, and bigger than pigs.

But of all the things my grandparents raised on the farm, vegetables were perhaps the most wondrous. Together they worked the soil, planting, growing, and nurturing beautiful and bountiful gardens filled with green beans, tomatoes, peppers, potatoes, purple hull peas, collard greens, and corn.

I didn't know it at the time, but my grandparents were among the last of a dwindling number of Black farmers in the 20th century. Accordingly, I grew up one of the few Black children in America who can remember what it's like to be fed fresh food that was never processed or passed through the hands of strangers and purchased at a grocery store. We got our food straight from our farm. This was a reality from which I and many subsequent generations of African Americans became further removed as we sought work and lives in metropolitan America.

As explained by blackdemographics.com: "In 1910, 89% of all African Americans still lived in the South, and 80% of them in rural areas ... By 1970, 47% of the nation's African Americans lived outside the South, and more than 80% were in urban areas."

Government data show just how much of a rarity my grandparents were as Black farmers. In 1920, there were nearly a million Black-owned farms in the United States. By 1964–when I was making those childhood trips to our farm on Fern Lake Road–the number had dropped to 184,004. By 2017, the number of Black farmers had dwindled to 35,470.

The reason behind the precipitous decline in the number of Black farmers is outlined in a September 2019 article titled "The Great Land Robbery: The shameful story of how 1 million black families have been ripped from their farms." It states:

"Owners of small farms everywhere, Black and white alike, have long been buffeted by larger economic forces. But what happened to Black landowners in the South, and particularly in the Delta, is distinct, and was propelled not only by economic change but also by white racism and local white power. A war waged by deed of title has dispossessed 98 percent of black agricultural landowners in America. They have lost 12 million acres over the past century. But even that statement falsely consigns the losses to long-ago history. In fact, the losses mostly occurred within living memory, from the 1950s onward.

Today, except for a handful of farmers ... who have been able to keep or get back some land, Black people in this most productive corner of the Deep South own almost nothing of the bounty under their feet."

Home Cooking

How my grandparents worked their farm was only part of the story of how I grew up eating farm-fresh food. The rest of it unfolded in my grandmother's kitchen. My grandmother's fried corn was second to none. She would painstakingly shave the tips of the kernels with her sharpest knife, then use a spoon to scrape and cull the fresh juiciness inside. That process is what made it so good. This kept the sometimes-tough outer skin of the kernels from getting stuck in your teeth. You just got the sweet and tender interior of the kernel.

She would coat her favorite, big, black, cast-iron skillet in oil and heat it. Next, she would carefully pour the creamy corn mixture, now enhanced with garden-fresh green peppers, into the soon-to-be sizzling, steamy, and bubbling pan. Sometimes she would add cheese and eggs; I'm still not quite sure if the goal was to add more flavor or to stretch the dish.

While I liked most vegetables okay, they were never the most appealing thing on the plate. I viewed vegetables rather practically–they were the things I had to eat to get dessert, more meat, or adult approval. I convinced myself that I liked sautéed okra. The praise for eating okra was especially high. Perhaps my grandparents were onto something. Research says eating okra has been shown to curtail stress, fatigue, and food cravings, among other benefits.

I ate most vegetables without objection. In my house, there were a few standards: yellow squash, always paired with onions; green beans and dark greens, especially turnips and collards, generally boiled for hours on end; all kinds of beans and peas; carrots, usually glazed with sugar and spices; pickled beets; and fried, boiled, baked, and mashed sweet and white potatoes.

Some folks from the South swear by fried green tomatoes, but the only fried vegetables in the Petties household were potatoes. I'm reasonably sure the only steamed vegetable I ever ate growing up was broccoli, which I loved, especially with cheese sauce. I never even heard of cauliflower, parsnips, or eggplant until I was an adult. I hated rutabagas, turnips, cabbage, and anything in the cabbage family, especially Brussels sprouts. No one was more surprised than me when I tasted oven-roasted rutabaga, turnips, and Brussels sprouts, as an adult – and liked them a lot. Once I had them chargrilled, I fell head over heels in love. As for mushrooms, I'm not sure if the first one I ever ate was camouflaged in cream of mushroom soup or hidden in a beef and mushroom pizza.

City Life

Once I went off to college and discovered fried zucchini, fried green tomatoes, fried mushrooms, and the dipping sauce that usually came with them, vegetables developed a bit more, shall we say, appeal. The vegetable experience started to get interesting and tasty. I soon lost the ability to appreciate vegetables for health reasons. Eventually, almost 100% of my eating was for pleasure and entertainment, not for nutrition. With the fresh vegetables of my childhood quickly forgotten, I was living a big city cosmopolitan life–or so I mistakenly thought.

Was I trying to forget my country upbringing and all that went along with it? I lost a true appreciation for vegetables and for the meaning of food in life. I often think of the countless times I said, "I want to eat something fun!" That generally meant Mexican food, something crunchy or fried, appetizers, snack, or finger food. Newsflash: spinach and artichoke dip with chips is not a vegetable. For forty-two years, I did not deliberately seek out the nutrition in vegetables, except maybe greens during the holidays or the occasional entrée salad. Here's what's so crazy: I managed to have this disrespectful view of vegetables while not being a regular meat-eater. No, I'm not a vegetarian. I have, however, practiced vegetarianism off and on over the past four decades, well before it was widely embraced by so many.

Early on, I was often asked, "If you don't eat meat, then what do you eat?" My reply was, "Everything else." While thinking to myself, "You can clearly tell by looking at me I don't have a problem finding food; that's the least of my problems."

Back to Basics

These days I eat and enjoy a wide variety of vegetables, but that has not always been my truth. For years, my go-to vegetable was a simple side salad, extra croutons, and blue cheese. I'm reasonably sure this is not what my grandmother had in mind with her dinnertime decree, "We always need something green on the plate."

Not that I had anything against vegetables, really. It's just that so much other food was more intriguing, more interesting, and different from the ordinary farm-raised vegetables of my youth. I did not view vegetables as intriguing, interesting, or exciting. I didn't see vegetables as being worldly or for having any kind of cachet. I never wanted to be plain or ordinary. Yes, I would proudly announce, "I'm a country girl," and then order bruschetta "extra drizzle of olive oil, please." But in many ways, I used food to distance myself from my small-town upbringing because in Marshall, Texas, bruschetta is a tomato sandwich.

While I cherished my formative years in Marshall, I wanted to move beyond that life. I got caught up in the Kool-Aid of big city stuff. The mistaken connections I made between food, the entertainment aspect of my profession, and the abundance of enticing food and drink available all the time led to my distorted view of food. I wanted everything in my life to be spectacular, including food. Consequently, food became a source of excitement. "I'll have the carrots." What's exciting about saying that?

It was during my own financial downturn that I discovered a new and glorious appreciation of vegetables. It now feels easy and natural, enjoying the simplicity of steamed rutabagas and the natural sweetness of char-grilled carrots—no glaze necessary. Roasted (or grilled) cauliflower and eggplant, smoked and chopped vegetable patties are divine. More importantly, I now look at vegetables with a new awareness and understanding. And as I figured out my new way of living, I opened my mind to new ways of returning to the vegetables I was raised on. The realization for me is that vegetables in and of themselves are extraordinary, especially Brussels sprouts with caramelized onions, pistachios, cranberries, and avocado oil. Yummy.

It's Not About the Food

It's About the Story Behind the Food

And I Would Love to Learn More About Your Food Story

FOOD STORY #6: FRESH OFF THE FARM

I am a country girl and proud of it. I boast that now. But I didn't always act or feel that way and it showed up in how I treated food and my body.

"I wanted everything in my life to be spectacular, including food. Consequently, food became a source of excitement. "I'll have the carrots." What's exciting about saying that?"

Do you have this skirt in a smaller size? Does saying that sound exciting?

Do you have a Food Story that you can share with me? michellep@leavinglarge.com

FOOD STORY 7

Living in the Past

LIVING IN THE PAST

O f all the gatherings that cause you to reflect on how much you've changed since you were young, nothing does the job quite like a high school reunion. And so, it was in 1986 as I prepared to attend my ten-year Marshall Senior High School reunion.

As far as my career was concerned, at twenty-eight I was in good shape. I had two years under my belt as an account executive for KDFW, the then-CBS affiliate in Dallas. I drove a brand-new white, five-speed Honda Prelude—which I parked in the two-car garage attached to my three-bedroom D.R. Horton garden-style home in Arlington, Texas. On top of that, I had paid off all my student loans.

When it came to my physical condition, that was an entirely different story. In fact, I had just learned during an appointment with a bariatric specialist that I was morbidly obese. Two-and-a-half years earlier I weighed 160 pounds; I now weighed 217.

Just like when my 6th grade teacher announced in front of the class during a routine weigh-in that I was 135 pounds, I was horrified. Only this time, I didn't respond to my weight the way I did when I was eleven, when I began to watch what I ate and ramped up my exercise. This time, the urgency of the situation and hearing the words "morbidly obese," had me follow the doctor's recommendations. Quite honestly, the doctor's promise of quick results held way more appeal than a gym membership. This meant showing up for a regimen of weekly weigh-ins, meetings, and appetite suppressing medication. My actions paid off. By reunion time, I was ready. I showed up in my new red and white box-pleated linen blend skirt ensemble, a respectable size 14. The entire outfit was a nod to my school colors and my year as a Marshall Senior High School cheerleader. Go Mavs!

Desperate Diets

Unfortunately, this would not be the last desperate diet that I went on just before a reunion. I did the same thing for both my 20-year and 40-year reunions. In 2006, I skipped my 30-year reunion because I had too much going on at the time, and the weight of it all was showing up in, well, my weight. When a few classmates asked if I was going to the reunion, I would lie, "I didn't get the notice until two weeks before, and it wasn't enough time for me to plan."

I could have easily gotten the information from classmates months earlier, had I really wanted to go. The truth is, 2006 was a very tough year for me and my weight was out of control. I was working my way through a myriad of unnamed stressors. This included retiring or being fired from my advertising sales job—depending on which version you heard. I also entered what I thought would be the lucrative world of mortgage financing. I was in the throes of renovating a 70-year-old house, with ever dwindling finances. And a longtime romance was finally imploding.

By the time I got wind of the upcoming reunion, I didn't have enough time to go on my pre-union crash diet. So, I didn't show up. I missed it. I wasn't feeling all that successful and I didn't want my classmates to see me in a career crisis, or, more significantly, so out of shape. I was embarrassed by my out-of-control body, which reflected an unraveling, out of control life.

Routines and Procedures

Hoping to avoid being a no-show for two high school reunions in a row, I started planning for my 40-year reunion early. Unlike the 30-year reunion, this time I was a few years into a stable relationship, with a chef, of all people. I was disciplined and vigilant about walking every day, even when it was rainy and cold, even when I didn't really feel like it. I played tennis regularly with my team, shout out to my Top Spinners. I hit the courts for 96 days straight, missing my 100-day goal by four days! I drank smoothies and protein drinks like they were going out of style, all to guard the body contouring effects of my 2013 breast reduction, tummy tuck, and thigh lift surgeries. I had convinced myself that if I had those procedures, they would ensure I never regain the fat, instead I would be motivated to lose even more.

Despite all those efforts, my weight was not budging. In fact, the weight seemed to creep back up, my body was fighting back by holding onto fat. That weight would not come off as easily as it had in my 20s, 30s, and 40s. Menopause and hormones are a real thing.

I was a size 16 squeezing into a 14. More importantly, my 40-year high school reunion was on the horizon. I was determined to go back looking good. So, I decided to seek reinforcements through liposuction—thighs, hips, and butt, then my arms. Success! Now I was a true size 14. I was ready to return. Deep down though, I still longed to be the size I was in 1993, when I felt I looked my best. Besides, I still had quite a few clothes from that time. Plus, I had purchased quite a few incentive outfits and planned to someday wear them. That was my secret goal: To get back to where I was. It dawned on me that most everybody has an "if I could just get back to where I was" dream. Maybe it's, "if I could just get back to how I looked before my first child was born" or "before my last child was born," or "before I went to college," "before menopause," "before I started this job," or "before I lost my job." Perhaps it's, "before the accident," "before the illness," "before my breakup," or "before my divorce."

Before, before, before.

Then I had a breakthrough. I realized I could not transform my situation physically, financially, or emotionally by desperately trying to recapture the past. That is, we cannot get the new by seeking the old.

I also realized that my reunion was more about me connecting with old friends and relishing memories we'd created together, and about me showing up, not the old version of me, but the real me.

It's Not About the Food

It's About the Story Behind the Food

And I Would Love to Learn More About Your Food Story

FOOD STORY #7: LIVING IN THE PAST

For years obesity robbed me of my ability to live in authenticity. Years of eating instead of expressing my truest feelings blocked my access to truly experiencing the present.

"By the time I got wind of the upcoming reunion, I didn't have enough time to go on my pre-union crash diet. So, I didn't show up. I missed it. I wasn't feeling all that successful and I didn't want my classmates to see me in a career crisis, or, more significantly, so out of shape. I was embarrassed by my out-of-control body, which reflected an unraveling, out of control life."

What special events and everyday occasions are you missing because of how you feel about your body?

Take a minute and share your Food Story with me: michellep@leavinglarge.com

FOOD STORY 8

The Flavor of Friendship

THE FLAVOR OF FRIENDSHIP

There was a time when I could eat Mexican food Monday through Saturday and twice on Sunday. In fact, there were occasions when that was exactly what I did. Man, it was all Mexican all the time. I don't think I ever met a Mexican restaurant I didn't like. I'm certain there was never a basket of chips or bowl of salsa that was ever safe in my presence.

When I think of how many bags of chips and how much salsa I have consumed in my lifetime, I am mortified. In the old days, it was perfectly routine for me to down a big bag or two of chips and salsa for breakfast, lunch, dinner or anytime. ¿Queso? ¿Guacamole? Even better. Nachos, quesadillas, fajitas, any kind of taco, jalapeños, enchiladas, tamales, flan, tres leches. They all gave new meaning to the phrase, "It's all good."

Resisting Mexican food, especially chips, was seemingly impossible for me. Just as Kryptonite sapped the strength of Superman, tortilla chips made me weak. It was pure torture to go for Mexican, order a meal, have a taco salad or tortilla soup, and not have three—I mean five, baskets of chips and salsa. More than once, I have gone to the store, bought three or four bags of stone ground, blue corn, tortilla chips—I deluded myself into believing they were healthier—and practically inhaled a bag in the car before I left the parking lot. Healthy choices be damned. I was forever the loser when it came to fightin' the feelin' so to speak. I guess you could safely say I was a Mexican foodaholic.

Venturing Out

It all started in 1976. I was a freshman at the University of Texas in Arlington, not quite as large as the main campus in Austin, but still daunting and formidable. In the space of three very short summer months, I had transitioned from my hometown of Marshall, Texas—a place of relative familiarity, popularity,

77

and certainty—to one where I felt awkward and unknown. Whatever the case, being at UTA was my ticket out. As much as I loved my grandparents, I couldn't wait to get out on my own and grab hold of an opportunity to expand my small-town sensibilities. The truth is, I had been dreaming of getting out of Marshall ever since I read my first Harlequin Romance. As much as I like to travel, if I had known there was such a thing as Foreign Service back then, well who knows?

College, for me, was never a question in my household—it was the natural order of things, a mandate if you will. My grandmother attended Wiley College, a small, private, historically Black liberal arts college in Marshall and once home to the debate team that inspired "The Great Debaters," the 2007 movie that starred Denzel Washington. She always regretted her decision not to "finish." My aunt and mother both graduated from the now long-defunct Bishop College, another historically Black college in Marshall, which closed in 1988 after moving to Dallas.

After growing up in a place that was home to not one but two historically Black colleges, where I knew everyone or their people and everybody knew me or my people, I now found myself in an unfamiliar college town. I delighted in the anonymity, independence, and the adventure of it all. Yet, there was a part of me that felt out of place, ill at ease, completely out of sync. That is, I felt too different. Still, I was committed to being who I was and who I was choosing to become.

An Unlikely Pair

While we did not start off as roommates, Bea and I became roommates during my sophomore year at UTA. In 1976, we were an unlikely pair. We were two chicks, one from the city, the other from the country, who met in the TV room of Lipscomb Hall (neither of us had a television in our room) and we bonded over our mutual distrust and disdain for Monica of General Hospital.

Our lengthy conversations went from soap operas to travel, family, books, food, movies, and baseball. Bea was a huge fan of baseball. Me? Not so much. But she liked talking about it, so I listened. One day Bea suggested that instead of eating dorm food that we eat dinner off campus. We hopped in her car and ended up in the parking lot of a Mexican restaurant called Dos Gringos. I had an immediate flashback to the humor and humiliation of my seventh-grade class trip to El Chico; but that's a story for another time.

Long after Bea and I finished our chicken and cheese enchiladas, like two old friends, we were still sitting, chatting, and swapping small town and big city stories. One basket of after-dinner-chips turned into two, then three, then four. They were free; why wouldn't two struggling college students get refills? Dos Gringos became our regular hangout. Chip after chip, week after week, semester after semester the chips kept on coming and we kept on talking, joking, laughing, and eating, flavors, fun, and friendship, indistinguishable. Any time either of us asked, "Hey, you up for Mexican?" The other one was always ready. There's nothing like hanging with your ride or die, and that's what Bea became, even after I moved away and long after our college years.

Chips in the Capital City

When I first moved to Washington, D.C. in the 80s, it was especially difficult to find what I considered good Mexican food. I was bereft until Texan George Bush was elected president and the Mexican food landscape changed, thank you Jesus! The fact is, even when I traveled to other cities, I scouted out the best places for Mexican cuisine, first.

Every time I go to a Mexican restaurant, it's not so much about anticipating and experiencing the intoxicating effect of a shot of Patron but wrapping myself in the memories and good times of a deep and abiding friendship.

When Bea came to visit me a few days for my birthday during the Covid-19 lockdown, we reminisced about Dos Gringos and Mexican food, but we didn't go out. Now forty-plus years later, this now not-so-unlikely pair—one a little younger, Black chick from the small town south and the other a little older, White chick from the big city north—are still the best of friends. And whenever I have Mexican food at home or out, I am immediately transported back to the early days of our friendship.

Over the years our friendship has evolved and grown in many ways, but in some ways, it has not changed one bit. The like-mindedness, the fun, the acceptance, the love, the everything that makes this friendship so special to me, has its roots in a Mexican restaurant. I realize now that it was never about the food; rather it was about the fun and flavor of the friendship that we share.

It's Not About the Food

It's About the Story Behind the Food

And I Would Love to Learn More About Your Food Story

FOOD STORY #8: FLAVOR OF FRIENDSHIP

Is it possible that the tortilla chips in Mexican restaurants are more addictive than crack? Would they be as addictive if they weren't free? It took me 40 years to determine that free is far too costly.

"Long after Bea and I finished our chicken and cheese enchiladas, like two old friends, we were still sitting, chatting, and swapping small town and big city stories. One basket of after-dinner-chips turned into two, then three, then four. They were free; why wouldn't two struggling college students get refills?

How long has your body been a casualty of the high cost of free food?

You can share your Food Story with me here: michellep@leavinglarge.com

FOOD STORY 9

Words with Friends

WORDS WITH FRIENDS

My grandmother, Mrs. Annie Mae Welch Petties, was a petite, soft-spoken Avon lady, "it's-the-quiet-ones-you-have-to-watch," fair-skinned woman, with longish "good hair" that she wore in a bun for many years. She was the epitome of classic, understated style. She knew a whole bunch of people all over town: her valued customers and her close friends, her crew.

Long before she was the Avon lady, my grandmother was a member of a close-knit group of women whose husbands all worked for Texas and Pacific Railway: Mrs. Clementine Matthews, Mrs. Virgie Lee Campbell, Mrs. Effie Mae Brown, and Mrs. Mary Ellen Edwards, along with Ms. Lula Mae Brown, Edna Lefall, and Ida Mae Jernigan. These were, by today's standards, my grandmother's BFFs. Over the years I watched intently as my grandmother cultivated, nourished, and cherished these abiding friendships. I saw and experienced firsthand the benefits of lifelong sisterhood and the value of having women in your life with whom you have a close bond, and why it is so important to have them. Afternoons or evenings these women would share a glass of tea or water on the porch or the "front room."

They enjoyed the blessing of their closeness as they laughed, talked, and solved the problems of the world. Just visiting. No food. Every unobstructed word deepened their bond. Absent distractions, it was pure "girl talk." Food was never central to their visits unless they were shelling peas.

In part, due to my grandmother's splendid example, I have a tribe—a tribe of smart, selfless, brilliant women whom I have the honor of calling friends. We work together. We shop till we drop together. We support each other in our collective and individual battles and victories. We meet over coffee, for breakfast, lunch, dinner, and happy hour. We also meet for weekend brunch.

Brunch. There is something marvelous and magical about the sound of that word, especially to a food addict like me. When I was growing up in the 60s and 70s, brunch was something White folks on TV did. For many years, at the mere mention of the word, I was front and center at the drop of a biscuit. I was an avowed brunch professional with decades of experience, spending my weekends discovering the best spot for bottomless mimosas and a waffle bar. Brunch, for me, meant happy times.

What is it about a brunch buffet that makes us lose our perspective and cause us to eat mass quantities of food? To eat so much that it's no longer pleasurable. To pile food onto one plate, instead of just going back for a second helping. Or to eat just because the food is there? I'm asking these questions as a reformed brunch buffet queen. So, is it about getting our money's worth or is it something else? Is it that, on some level, we have come to believe that more is better?

I have not been to an all-you-can-eat-buffet in years. To think, once upon a time brunch was an excuse to ring in the weekend, celebrate holidays, birthdays, weddings, and baby showers, or for no reason at all. That is, it was a calorie-laden, high priced status symbol, evidence that I could afford the good life like the White folks on television. Symbolism aside, brunch allows my sister circle to go beyond and build friendships; that is, if we don't blow the opportunity. If we don't get so ensnared by the food before us that we totally miss the moment or lose the intention for the occasion or the person.

Today, I have a much different perspective about brunch. I'd rather spend that time on the tennis court. I'm no longer caught up in the brunch life nor do I view it as portal to prestige. I now prefer to focus on my friends and the moments we have together, not the food.

A few months ago, I met one of my tribe for drinks. During the conversation, she commented about my new attitude toward food and how I was different. She went on to explain that the first time we met for a meal "you never looked up from your plate." I was devastated by her comment. I tried to tell her that it wasn't true. She assured me that it was. I was appalled to think I had gone to lunch with her and showed more interest in the food than in her, a person. In that moment I felt an immense sense of loss, like I had robbed her and myself. I also felt tremendous sadness because I knew deep down, she was telling the truth.

I thought of all the decades of meals where I missed important personal connections because I was focused on the food and not the person in front of me. And I knew for certain, if I had done that to her, I had done it to many others.

Food, at that time, was not a connector; it was a separator and barrier to authentic communication. Yes, we can connect over food. Yes, we can bond over food. Why else do we like to hang out in the kitchen during house parties? Food is our source. Isn't that why the kitchen is known as the heart of the home? Why do designer kitchens drive up home values? Food is life. Food is creation. Good food mixed with good friends is all good. Not ever did my grandmother and her friends meet for brunch. From time to time, they sat on porches and shelled pecans or picked greens. They talked a bit after church on Sunday afternoons. They quilted together and shared canned figs. The value they found was in each other, unearthed as they spent precious time together. I have finally found it, as well.

Once I realized that precious time together was the tie that binds, food became an afterthought and not the centerpiece. Interestingly, that's also when the scale began moving in a downward direction.

It's Not About the Food

It's About the Story Behind the Food

And I Would Love to Learn More About Your Food Story

FOOD STORY #9: WORDS WITH FRIENDS

If I had a dollar for the number of times I have said, "Let's meet for lunch." or "Let's meet for dinner." or "Let's meet for drinks." We live in a time when friends and food are almost synonymous, all you can eat, all you can drink, with all your besties and life is good. But what happens bonding over brunch leads to a breach?

"I was appalled to think I had gone to lunch with her and showed more interest in the food than in her, a person. In that moment I felt an immense sense of loss, like I had robbed her and myself. I also felt immense sadness because I knew deep down, she was telling the truth."

Which is more important, who you eat with or where you go to eat?

Do you have a Food Story that you want to share?
michellep@leavinglarge.com

FOOD STORY 10

Hula Hoop Dreams

HULA HOOP DREAMS

emember hula hoops? When I was growing up in the 1960s, it seemed like everyone in my neighborhood had these giant looping circles of colorful plastic. Kids would be doing the hula hoop not just on their waists, but with their necks, knees, legs, and arms. They would even use the hula hoop like a jump rope. It looked like they were having tons of fun. But no hula hoop for Michelle. At least I never got to have one of my own. It wasn't that my grandparents, who raised me, couldn't afford to buy one. After all, hula hoops only cost about two dollars, if that. Besides, I had plenty of other toys: jump ropes, jacks, a bicycle, beach balls, and beaucoup Barbie dolls. I even had the Black Barbie. Truth be told, I had just about any toy that a young girl needed to be happy. I even had an entire swing set in my backyard. But, when it came to the hula hoop, my grandmother said "no" when I begged for a hula hoop of my own. Adding, "You're way too big for a hula hoop."

Downward Spiral

I know my grandmother loved me. I know she meant well. But hearing those harsh words as a child was too much. I was devastated. Those words were the seeds for my deep-seated, self-limiting, subconscious belief that I was too big to experience the simple pleasures available to others.

It was hard enough not being good at doing the hula hoop and seeing all the other kids get longer turns than I because they could hula hoop so much better. But my grandmother's words paved the way for a vicious cycle of thinking: If I was "too big" for a hula hoop and was never going to get one of my own, then I had to find other ways to make myself happy. So, I turned to food for comfort and pleasure. Maybe it would be an extra helping of peach cobbler or an extra scoop of ice cream. Of course, all those desserts came with heavy consequences. And I do mean heavy. By the time I was in the 6th grade, I weighed 135 pounds. Soon my biggest issue was not that I couldn't have a hula hoop, but that I couldn't wear the same clothes as other kids because they didn't make them my size. So, I had to wear "stout girls" clothes. I even wore a girdle. Nor did it help that I was always the biggest kid on my block or in my class.

Wrong and Right Remedy

There are two cruel ironies to this story. The first is that one of the reasons I was overfed in the first place is because my grandparents—God bless them—wanted to make sure I was never hungry. I was born two months premature, and my grandparents reminded me until the day I left for college that I was a "seven-month baby" so they needed to make sure I always got plenty to eat. In their minds, the fact that I was a "stout" kid was evidence that they had "saved" me. After all, I was born underweight and premature. I guess having seen me at such a tiny size at birth made such a jarring impression on them that they felt like they had to overcompensate to make sure I grew up healthy. The problem was their definition of healthy.

The second irony is that if I had gotten a hula hoop, it could have possibly helped me lose weight or at least not get as big as I did. Research suggests that doing the hula hoop for just a half hour can help burn some serious calories. Consider this article from howstuffworks.com. So, does slinging a hula hoop around your waist provide a decent workout? You bet your abs it does. A 2011 study sponsored by the American Council on Exercise put 16 women between the ages of 16 and 59 to the test. The participants averaged 151 heart beats per minute, burning 7 calories a minute, or about 210 calories during a half hour of hooping. To put that in perspective, the average 154-pound (70-kilogram) person burns approximately 220 calories during a half hour of heavy yard work or vigorous weightlifting.

It's important to note that the study was based on a thirty-minute aerobics routine that involves twirling weighted hula hoops around the waist, arms, and legs.

Black Women and Hula Hoops

These days, there's a plethora of examples of Black women who have embraced the hula hooping to stay in shape. Some of them are quite prominent. For instance, back in 2009, "Forever" First Lady Michelle Obama once decided to "hoop it up for health" on the South Lawn of the White House as part of her effort to keep America's kids healthy and fit.

Then there's Marawa the Amazing, a circus performer known as the "World Conquering Hula Hoop Master." When Marawa was asked if hula hoop workouts were underrated, she replied that they were "100% the most underrated. It's literally the greatest full body workout of all time," Marawa said. "I will teach you!"

Unfortunately, I didn't have Michelle Obama or Marawa the Amazing to tell my grandmother that I was not too big for a hula hoop, that I was actually too big not to have one! Had I been allowed a hula hoop I might have escaped many of the challenges that I endured as a child and as an adult as I struggled to get control over my eating habits and my weight.

That's all in the past now. We, however, can learn from our past and create a better future. I am here to tell you that life is way more fun for me at 158 pounds than it was at 258 pounds. And—unlike when I was a chubby child—I can now wear all, and I do mean all, the stylish clothes I want to wear.

It's Not About the Food

It's About the Story Behind the Food

And I Would Love to Learn More About Your Food Story

FOOD STORY #10: HULA HOOP DREAMS

I spent decades desperate for a way to feel comfortable in my own skin.

"Unfortunately, I didn't have Michelle Obama or Marawa the Amazing to tell my grandmother that I was not too big for a hula hoop, that I was actually too big not to have one! Had I been allowed a hula hoop I might have escaped many of the challenges that I endured as a child and as an adult as I struggled to get control over my eating habits and my weight."

What scenarios make you feel self-conscious about your weight?

Does this story remind you of a Food Story that you can share?
michellep@leavinglarge.com

FOOD STORY 11

Food for the Fourth

FOOD FOR THE FOURTH

B arbecuing and the Fourth of July go hand in hand for Black folks. And so, it was for me growing up in the 1960s in Marshall, Texas. My earliest memories of those big community cookouts on the Fourth of July originated at a place we knew as Cole's Farm. People from all parts of East Texas and beyond would come to this cookout for the best barbecue, finest liquor, and just an overall good time.

If you wanted to commit a crime in the Marshall area, the Fourth of July would have been the best day to do it because all the law enforcement officers in Marshall and the surrounding area would be chowing down at Cole's.

A Family Affair

The man behind this annual gathering was Big Cole. At least that's how most people knew Clifford Cole, a big, towering, bellowing, no-nonsense, workhorse of a man who owned and operated Cole's Garage and Wrecker Service.

Big Cole and his wife, Miss Pearlie, the parents of one of my best friends, monitored area police scanners 24/7 for accidents and people in distress. If you saw him, usually it was when he was in his signature army green tow truck, headed to save someone in distress. Rescuing people from ditches and car wrecks was part of their life's work and enabled them to build a thriving enterprise.

If it made sense for anyone among us to celebrate by barbecuing on Independence Day, it made sense for Big Cole and Miss Pearlie, who were truly independent thanks to their business.

But they weren't arrogant about it. They knew their business thrived only because of the automotive mishaps and misfortunes suffered by people in the community. So, every Fourth of July, Big Cole would turn his farm into a place of celebration to show his gratitude and appreciation for the many customers who enabled his business to grow and flourish.

Growth, Gorging, and Gluttony

As his business grew, so did the Cole's annual Fourth of July cookout. Year after year, more and more people showed up—family, friends, and folks who became friends because of a common experience: Big Cole had saved them. It was a truly joyous occasion, one that resonates with me to this day. But as much as the annual Fourth of July barbecue at Big Cole's farm represented a celebration of friendship and family, good times, gratitude, generosity, and hospitality, there was another side to it. I now see it, as I look back with the wisdom that comes from consciousness.

Each Fourth of July we all got to enjoy a fantastic feast; in reality, those who attended this annual event, myself included, treated it more like a pig-out than a cookout. It was a time when you could eat all the food you wanted for as long as you wanted–and that's exactly what most of us did.

On the one hand, perhaps our gluttony could be forgiven. You see, you haven't really had barbecue until you've had the kind that comes from East Texas. And of all the barbecue in East Texas, none was better than what rolled off the custom-built barbecue pit on Cole's Farm. This is something of which I have firsthand knowledge. My Aunt Dorothy and Miss Pearlie, the best of friends, worked on that giant sized smoking pit from sunup to sundown, continually basting and turning big juicy slabs of pork ribs, chicken, burgers, hot dogs, and brisket.

The barbecue sauce? Well, let's just say people always wanted extra. There were plenty of other things to eat at this massive spread: potato salad, deviled eggs, corn, baked beans, all kinds of snacks, and an array of homemade desserts. The grownups had plenty of adult beverages and the kids had plenty of grape and strawberry soda. That was the one day when no one really monitored how much soda we drank, a budding sugar addict's paradise.

The most fun I ever had growing up was at these barbecues. There were horses, hayrides, and tractor pulls to keep the most active kid entertained. Fireworks and fun were the words of the day as we ran and laughed. For us kids, this event was among the crown jewels of all summer activities, right up there with a trip to AstroWorld—the famous but since-demolished amusement park in Houston that paid homage to the city's early role as a hub of human space flight.

Zero Gravity Environment

We may not have been astronauts in training at Cole's Farm, but we sure acted like we floated in space. It was a time when we could be carefree—when we could eat with our hands, lick our fingers, get our clothes dirty, run around, and be loud and rambunctious. It was a day when we didn't have to think about the cares of the world or anyone else's because everything was okay. It was a day when we could abandon all rules about eating. It was a day when everything was everything, and there was plenty of it. It was a celebration of plenty, of good times and of sharing. It was a time when I ate and ate, with little thought to the consequences because the hotdogs and the hayrides were all wrapped up in the same experience.

Better Discipline

Over the years, I attended countless barbecues, cookouts, and picnics. As an adult, I continued to eat with the same no rules, no consequences, and wild abandon of a kid on Big Cole's Farm. A kid who could not distinguish food from fun. The food became fun. It was a time that I couldn't tell myself no, even if I wanted to. Certainly not with so many friends and family around. What else was there to do but overeat, drink, and be merry? It was food, festivities, and fun all rolled into one.

My battle to quiet my insatiable desire for food used to be real. I have since learned that it's possible to have the kind of carefree abandon and no holds barred fun that I experienced growing up without falling into a food frenzy. Now, it's all about clarity.

These days, food is less about fun and more about fueling my body. Now, I don't have to pig out at barbecues and picnics; I simply bask in my memories of those childhood Fourth of July cookouts.

Just for the record—whether it's spelled BBQ, Bar-B-Que, or Barbecue—none of it compares to the East Texas BBQ at Big Cole's Farm.

It's Not About the Food

It's About the Story Behind the Food

And I Would Love to Learn More About Your Food Story

FOOD STORY #11: FOOD FOR THE FOURTH

Daily, we are bombarded, with messages telling us
that food and entertainment are synonymous.

"As an adult, I continued to eat with the same no rules, no consequences, and wild abandon of a kid on Big Cole's Farm. A kid who
could not distinguish food from fun. The food became the fun."

Please share your picnic - cookout Food Story
here: michellep@leavinglarge.com

FOOD STORY 12

When Cinnamon Rolls Call

WHEN CINNAMON ROLLS CALL

My love for cinnamon rolls goes back to the days when my cousins Bernard and Pettis would call me on the phone to let me know that my Aunt Dorothy was making a batch in her kitchen. She lived about a mile away from my grandparents' home.

"Momma's making cinnamon rolls!" They would whisper over the phone.

This was always a big deal to us. So big that whenever my cousins alerted me, I would find a way to make my way over to their house because I knew we were about to have a good time.

My cousins and I would gather in the kitchen, eagerly watching as my aunt, a longtime master pastry maker for the Marshall Independent School District, plied her culinary skills to produce what would ultimately become my favorite pastry of all time. Cinnamon rolls, especially after Cinnabon stores became ubiquitous at airports and shopping malls across the United States, would become my nemesis. It was something that I would not defeat until much later in life.

The foundation for my Cinnabon habit was laid during those cinnamon roll-making sessions in Aunt Dorothy's kitchen, where my cousins and I would stand in eager anticipation and argue over who would get to lick the spoon.

Cinnamon rolls were far from the only thing that this master pastry-maker for the local school district used to make. The same treats that Aunt Dorothy made for the kids at school she made for us at home, only better. Every day was like a holiday at her house. There was always a beautiful caramel cake—hands down everybody's favorite—or double boiler banana pudding, sweet potato pie, pecan pie, or fruit cobbler. And if we were in good favor, all the stars were aligned, and it had been a while since she had thrown a shoe at us or threatened us with a Hot Wheels track for misbehaving, she would make her special cinnamon rolls. Which, I must say, were ten times better than any Cinnabon I've ever tasted. If only my aunt had started a franchise to sell her cinnamon rolls, this small-town pastry chef might have become a millionaire; and Aunt Dorothy's cinnamon rolls would be known worldwide.

My Battle with Cinnabons

I was in my 30s when I tasted a Cinnabon for the first time. I treated myself to this heavenly confection during an all-day shopping extravaganza at a shopping mall. Long before I actually saw them, the distinct, familiar, and intoxicating aromas of cinnamon, flour, powdered sugar, and sweet butter drew me near. The first bite was paradise. The out-of-this-world sweetness of cream cheese icing. The sugar-sweetened Makara cinnamon swirled throughout the bun. The tender, moist, gooey center, and the stick-to-your-fingers goodness! Cinnabons were good, damn near as good as the ones my Aunt Dorothy used to make.

They were close enough!

I gobbled up the first one, then another one immediately afterwards. I remember my skinny shopping companion saying, "I can get one, but, oh my God, I can't eat it all at one time. It's way too rich!" I had no idea what "too rich" meant. I could not relate. I knew exactly what way too good meant. Can't eat the whole thing? In my mind, the question was, "How can you not eat the whole thing?"

I was hooked. Soon, I couldn't walk by a Cinnabon kiosk without buying a half dozen with extra frosting. Eventually, I planned my weekend shopping expeditions only at malls where I knew Cinnabons were sold. As if selling them in malls wasn't enough, the company had the nerve to start selling them in grocery stores and airports.

Sugar, Cravings, and Memories

My cravings for Cinnabons undoubtedly had something to do with my desire to return to the warmth and comfort of Aunt Dorothy's kitchen. Physically I might have been in a mall shopping, but as soon as I inhaled cinnamon and cream cheese I was transported back in time to those lovely days when my cousins and I eagerly awaited my aunt's cinnamon rolls.

Chasing the sweetness of a memory, I've eaten more Cinnabons than I can count. I had it bad. I was a stone-cold sugar addict who was so obese that insurance companies refused to cover me. At close to 1000 calories, eating just one Cinnabon a week was responsible for an extra twelve pounds a year.

When I figured out that my sugar addiction, compulsions, and cravings were linked to specific, pleasurable memories, I realized that I was hungry not for the food itself but for the feeling I associated with the food. Prior to that, I had no idea this was going on. For years, instead of finding joy in my memories, I mistook my emotional cravings as physical hunger. In reality, I was hungry for something that food could not supply – warmth, love, comfort, and family.

Kicking the Habit

I'm not sure exactly when I stopped bingeing on Cinnabons, but I remember finally realizing that I could savor the memory without eating the food. Now when I walk by a Cinnabon counter, there's no urge, no craving, no pull. I think less about Aunt Dorothy's kitchen—the aromas of cinnamon, sugar, flour, and vanilla that always hung in the air—and more about what a missed business opportunity it was for her. Then again, if my Aunt Dorothy had turned her cinnamon rolls into a franchise, she would have contributed to America's problem with food, not something I'd want for her.

It's Not About the Food

It's About the Story Behind the Food

And I Would Love to Learn More About Your Food Story

FOOD STORY #12: WHEN CINNAMON ROLLS CALL

Superman had his Kryptonite. And for years
and years, Cinnabons were mine.

"I remember my skinny shopping companion saying, "I can get one,
but, oh my God, I can't eat it all at one time. It's way too rich!" I had
no idea what "too rich" meant. I could not relate. I knew exactly
what way too good meant. Can't eat the whole thing? In my mind,
the question was, "How can you not eat the whole thing?""

When you are feeling down and alone, what
food do you find yourself craving?

Can you share a Food Story about your favorite pastry?
michellep@leavinglarge.com

FOOD STORY 13

The Cake is in the Mail

THE CAKE IS IN THE MAIL

L ike many young children, I grew up with a great love for the things my mother used to bake. The difference was I didn't grow up with my mother.

The affinity I developed for my mother's baking came about during the 1960s and 70s while growing up with my grandparents in Marshall, Texas, a small city near the Texas-Louisiana border, where my grandparents owned a farm on the outskirts of town.

Oh, sure, there was always plenty of good food—good soul food—to eat from the family farm: sweet potatoes and collard greens. Chicken and dumplings. Pecan pie and peach cobbler. But none of those things could compare to the one thing that would always bring my grandparents and me so much joy every holiday season between Thanksgiving and Christmas. That one thing was: The Box.

For weeks, the house would fill with excited anticipation about the box. When my grandmother would finally announce that Sara Jean had put the box in the mail—Sara Jean was my mother—the anticipation would build even more.

We all looked forward to the arrival of the box. Even my grandfather, a retired railman from the old Texas and Pacific Railroad, a church trustee and a former bootlegger who was known to gamble on Saturday nights, eagerly looked forward to the box. In those days, not too much excited my grandfather, at least not that I knew of.

There was no FedEx or Amazon back then. So, sometimes the box would come by bus. Going to the bus station to pick it up was a big deal. We'd all climb into my grandfather's pickup truck, or my grandmother's pale green 1960s Chevy Bel Air, and go downtown to the Continental Trailways Bus Station to pick up the box.

Between the time when my mother called to say the box was on its way and its actual arrival, my grandparents would warmly recall my mother's wide-ranging adventures. I listened intently, hanging on to their every word, soaking up every detail. My mother's essence filled us even before the box arrived.

Day after day during the holiday season I would ask, "Is the box coming today?" My grandmother would always pacify me with something like, "We'll see" or "It's on its way."

When the box finally arrived, it would be neatly wrapped in plain brown paper. There was so much joy in just opening the box—lots of oohing and aahing as we wondered what was beneath the precise folds of aluminum foil.

As soon as we opened the box, beautiful aromas of cranberry bread, fruit cake, banana bread, lemon pound cake, and my mother filled the room. I remember the pleasure of deeply inhaling the distinct combination of my mother's scent and the vanilla and spice she used to bake her cakes.

As the cakes were unveiled, I beamed with pride knowing my mother had made the brown, golden mounds that I wanted to gobble up on the spot. Almost immediately, my grandmother would be on the phone telling anyone who would listen about the box of goodies that Sara Jean had sent. One of my mother's cakes would be prominently placed on display under a glass cake dome. So, for a short while—at least until the last piece of cake was gone—that glass cake dome would serve as the centerpiece for our dining room table. And why shouldn't it? When my mother sent us those homemade baked goods, she was sending us her love.

It's not that my mother wasn't able or willing to care for me. She, however, lived during a time when society wasn't so accepting of an unmarried woman having a child. Plus, my mother was a schoolteacher. Even today, teachers may lose their jobs if they do something that the community deems unacceptable. Sixty years ago, having a child out-of-wedlock most certainly would have cost my mother her teaching position. So, she did what a lot of unmarried women and young girls did back then when they got pregnant, she went away. Then my family did what many families did and said she had gotten "sick." So, my mother went away and had me. Once she had me, my family's story was that she had "gotten well."

My grandparents kept me. They kept me, loved me, and let my mother live her life. As time went on, they along with my mother decided it was best that they formally adopt me. I didn't understand or know this growing up. All I knew was that I missed my mother, and I loved her dearly.

When she sent those cakes, eating them and enjoying them was my way of reconnecting with my mother. That's how I tried to fill that void. Which is why I would go back, sometimes sneak back, for slice after slice—until it was all gone. Eating my mother's cakes was an attempt to keep myself filled with that joy. For a long time, there was an empty space inside me for my mother, a space I held open long after she passed in 1981. Now I realize that for many years I tried in vain to fill the emptiness with food, pound cake, and other addictions. Thankfully, that emptiness was finally healed years ago. But make no mistake about it, only after a lot of counseling and therapy was I able to come to terms with why my mother didn't raise me.

Now, I am full of understanding, compassion, and gratitude for the selflessness my mother demonstrated by allowing my grandparents to raise me. And, of course, I have fond memories of the cakes my mother used to make.

It's Not About the Food

It's About the Story Behind the Food

And I Would Love to Learn More About Your Food Story

FOOD STORY #13: THE CAKE IS IN THE MAIL

I was mad, sad, and resigned to the fact that I would
never be allowed to live with my mother.

"When she sent those cakes, eating them and enjoying them was
my way of reconnecting with my mother. That's how I tried to fill
that void. Which is why I would go back, sometimes sneak back,
for slice after slice—until it was all gone. Eating my mother's
cakes was an attempt to keep myself filled with that joy."

Are you unconsciously trying to fill an imaginary hole with food?

You can share a Food Story about your mother's special
dessert here: michellep@leavinglarge.com

FOOD STORY 14

Adkisson Adventure

ADKISSON ADVENTURE

Of the many things I used to do with my mother whenever she came to visit us in Marshall, my all-time favorite was when we'd both slip off to the local fabric stores for a few hours. My mom had a knack for making clothes. I think she could have easily become a fashion designer if she had really wanted to pursue that career. She was often called upon to make outfits for people she knew, everyone from family and friends to her fellow teachers and military wives, stateside and abroad. She got her talent from her mother and passed it down to me.

Our shared passion led to many fun trips to fabric stores such as Hancock Fabrics, where we would get lost in time as we blissfully flipped through giant Vogue and Butterick pattern books and dreamt up fanciful runway projects and fashions. It was a way to keep our bond strong even though my grandparents had adopted me to spare my mother – a schoolteacher – the difficulties that would arise during those days, from having a child outside of marriage.

A Seamstress' Paradise

None of that mattered as we would roam the aisles rummaging through colorful bolts of fabric and a dizzying array of buttons, snaps, and trim. We found ourselves drawn to bargain tables loaded with jumbled remnants of cloth. If there was such a thing as a seamstress's paradise, this was it.

One of the most memorable of these fabric store excursions took place in 1972. On the way home, while driving along Pinecrest Drive and nearing the end of our time together, my mother caught a glimpse of a sign to what for her was a familiar place.

"Adkisson Donut Shop," the sign declared. "Made Fresh Daily!"

"I haven't been there in years," my mother said.

I had never been there, even though I had passed that small, nondescript storefront countless times.

"Oh, they have the best donuts!" my mother whispered, as if she were about to let me in on a big secret.

As soon as we stepped inside the Adkisson Donut Shop, we were greeted by the beautiful, sugar-wrapped aromas of yeast, flour, and bubbling canola oil that owned the air. Trays lined with light puffy wheels of plain or glazed, lemon, and chocolate-infused delicacies filled the display cases. There were donut holes, cinnamon apple fritters, and an array of donuts in varying degrees of completion, some rising, some lightly cooking in the fryers and floating to the top, others draining and waiting to be iced or filled. I found myself fascinated by the complexities of constructing the delicate confection.

My mother bought a dozen donuts and holes for us to take home to eat for breakfast the next day. Well, some of those treats didn't survive until the next day. Once we got back in the car, my mother immediately dug into the plain white packaging and pulled out one of the delicious pastries.

"Oh, these are good," she sang as we shared one of the donuts. She could see from the look on my face that I–now a willing coconspirator in her donut indulgence – certainly agreed.

Secret Spot

The experience proved to be one of the most delightful of my childhood. But was it truly delightful? Or did I think it was because it involved my mother sharing this one thing with me that she liked so much, her secret sweet spot? Whatever the reason, I got caught up. Did my sugar addiction begin here? Or did this experience just fuel it? Years later, I discovered I was addicted to sugar. More significantly, I was emotionally addicted to the memory of this sweet moment with my mother.

This "Adkisson Adventure," if you will, lingered in my spirit long after my mother packed up my brothers and sister and returned to her home in Wichita Falls. So, to recapture the moment, whenever I would get my allowance or extra money, I would walk or ride my bike two miles to that donut shop just to relive the experience. Looking back on that time, I believe one of the reasons the grown-woman-me would often eat a dozen donuts was not that I didn't have self-control, discipline, or willpower to overcome my sugar addiction. But rather, I was craving the pleasurable memory of being with my mother.

The memory is still fresh–just like the donuts advertised by Adkisson. It may have led me to devour more donuts than anyone ever should. I have no regrets though, because those Adkisson donuts were something my mother shared with me because she loved me and wanted nothing more than to see me happy.

It's Not About the Food

It's About the Story Behind the Food

And I Would Love to Learn More About Your Food Story

FOOD STORY #14: ADKISSON ADVENTURE

I was out of balance, eating for pleasure only.
It was a slippery, sugary slope.

"Whatever the reason, I got caught up. Did my sugar addiction begin here? Or did this experience just fuel it? Years later, I discovered I was addicted to sugar. More significantly, I was emotionally addicted to the memory of this sweet moment with my mother."

When did you learn that refined sugar is not food?

Do you have a sugar related Food Story that you would like to share?
michellep@leavinglarge.com

FOOD STORY 15

Bus Station Goodbyes

BUS STATION GOODBYES

T wo weeks before my 62nd birthday, I tested out a pair of small white summer pants that I purchased for motivation. I, however, discovered they were a tad tight. Up until then, I had been diligent and vigilant about my eating and exercise habits and diet. I had gotten down to 160 pounds after having been 215; I was looking and feeling good. I was almost slim enough to wear those white pants, but not quite. I really felt I should have been able to wear them, but I could not. "Oh well," I said to myself. "I'll just keep doing what I'm doing. I'll get there. A little slower than I want, but I've been on this new road for a while. I'll get there," I reassured myself.

About thirty minutes later, I thought to myself, "Ooh, I want some ice cream. Some ice cream would really be good right about now." This thought was a bit surprising to me. It had been months since I had given ice cream a second thought. Where did this old craving come from? I also remember thinking, "I could not possibly be hungry. I just ate less than an hour ago." I was also intelligent enough to know that a big scoop of Häagen-Dazs certainly wouldn't get me any closer to fitting into those summer pants for my birthday. I was trying to understand where this specific desire for ice cream was coming from. I sat with the question for a while.

Waistline Woes

The culprit? Those white summer pants.

Let me explain. Unexpressed disappointment, frustration, and a bit of sadness about not fitting into those summer pants triggered those cravings. The more I thought about it, the impulse to turn to the cool and sweet smoothness of ice cream to soothe the sadness was not a big surprise. In fact, it made perfect sense!

Ice cream represented some of my fondest childhood memories. I was raised by my loving grandparents, away from my mother, brothers, and sister who lived in Wichita Falls, Texas. Although my mother lived in another city, she was always within reach. It was routine for her to pack up my brothers and sister and show up at the bus station in Marshall for us to pick them up along with all their bags. It was always a great treat for me when they came to visit. I would get so excited. My grandparents would just light up because my mother, Sara Jean, their daughter, the favorite and youngest of their four children, was coming home for a visit with grands in tow.

Whether they stayed for a week or weekend, the visits were always much too short. We would have to take my mother, brothers, and sister back to the bus station for their trip back home, our little interlude over, until the next time.

Palatable Partings

We had a bus station ritual that made their departure, though sad, a little easier. I now understand the meaning of bittersweet. I understand how "parting is such sweet sorrow." The sorrow of our parting was sweetened by our customary trip to the Marshall Creamery, which was located across the street from the bus station. Every trip back, we would leave the house early enough to have time for ice cream before the bus departed. Not just any ice cream though, but "gourmet before it was gourmet" ice cream from the hometown creamery just a few sweet steps away. There were freshly churned, hand-dipped flavors not commonly found in the local Brookshire's or Safeway grocery store in the 70s, like black cherry and butter pecan. Giant scoops for twenty-five cents. My mother and all her kids, including me, sat on the stoop in front of the creamery laughing, joking, and talking, creating a sweet memory before saying our final goodbyes.

The bus would come much too soon; their visit would be over, and things would go back to normal. The bittersweetness of the goodbyes would linger long after the bus departed. In her wisdom, my mother knew the joy and pleasure we received from her special ice cream treat would take the sting out of their leaving for all of us, even her.

Often, I would ride my bike or walk by the bus station, intentionally. I would look over at the creamery and feel us. I could see us. I could hear us. A mother and her four children. I would smile and recall the ice cream moments. Sweet! Who wouldn't want to relive those precious moments over and over—especially in times of stress? Who wouldn't want to be wrapped up in yesterday's memories and relive the warmth of being loved? Who, in their right mind, would not want to relive those moments many times over?

Cream, Cones, and Consciousness

Yes, I mistakenly thought it was the ice cream that caused me to savor those precious moments whenever my family left. I didn't realize that the ice cream was really the icing on the delicious cake of enjoying my mother, sister, and brothers, with whom I did not live. Yet, they influenced my life immeasurably. The times we spent together cemented our relationship. It was family, not the ice cream, that made me feel loved.

I must say, there's something about the innocence and purity of the moment that makes you smile when you're just sitting, talking, and eating ice cream. It's something about that smooth, silky, delicate sweetness that makes you forget about everything else that's going on and just be in the present moment.

In life, there's always something going on. There's always something to be stressed about. And I don't have to say it, but I will; you cannot escape stress with ice cream. To be quite honest, there were times when a half-gallon of ice cream was the only thing that could make me smile or happy, times when I craved companionship and ice cream was the next best thing. People don't generally sit down intending to eat a half-gallon of ice cream. Yet sometimes they do; and it can happen one bowl at a time.

As I process this memory, a kind of peace settles over me. I no longer feel like I am fighting with myself. I'm not struggling. Now I can savor the memories without craving the food that inspired the memory. I no longer feel like a visitor in a body that I've borrowed. There is no imposter in my body. I feel like I own my body. I know that peace with my body is imminent. No, I am not quite there yet, but I know it's just around the corner. What is peace to me? I experience peace as I change what food means to me when food cravings no longer dictate what I eat and how I live.

Confident, I look at the still-too-tight white summer pants, sure that I will absolutely wear them by my 62nd birthday. Yes, of this, I am sure.

It's Not About the Food

It's About the Story Behind the Food

And I Would Love to Learn More About Your Food Story

FOOD STORY #15: BUS STATION GOODBYES

Sometimes you must sit with the craving. That's the secret.

"About thirty minutes later, I thought to myself, "Ooh, I want some ice cream. Some ice cream would really be good right about now." This thought was a bit surprising to me. It had been months since I had given ice cream a second thought. Where did this old craving come from? I also remember thinking, "I could not possibly be hungry. I just ate less than an hour ago." I was also intelligent enough to know that a big scoop of Häagen-Dazs certainly wouldn't get me any closer to fitting into those summer pants for my birthday."

Why am I craving this? Now?

Please share your favorite ice cream Food Story
with me: michellep@leavinglarge.com

FOOD STORY 16

Crème De La Crème

CRÈME DE LA CRÈME

My love affair with ice cream began in Compton, California, in the summer of 1962. I was staying with my Aunt Baby Doll. We lived on West Poplar Street.

Like just about any urban neighborhood back in those days, pandemonium would ensue whenever the melodious tunes of the ice cream truck could be heard off in the distance. It was fair warning for all the kids within earshot to go collect whatever spare change they could get. The ice cream man was coming.

Neighborhood kids would lose their minds, racing home to get money from their mothers and then back outside to the much-anticipated, ice cream truck. Everyone had their coins ready, one thin dime the only thing standing between them and Nutty Buddy nirvana. After they bought the cold and creamy confection of their choice, kids would run around, singing and dancing with happiness. But not me.

It wasn't because I wasn't quick enough. I was never the fastest kid on the block, but I ran home fast enough to ask Aunt Baby Doll for whatever coins she could spare to make my ice cream dreams come true.

The reason I missed out on the ice cream truck experience is because of a conversation that went something like this:

Me: (Frantic and excited) Quick, I need money. I need ten cents!

Aunt Baby Doll: (Cooler than the coolest of cool breezes) Why do you need ten cents?

Me: The ice cream man is outside. Hurry! He's gonna leave!

I'm dumbfounded as to why she is asking me this question. She had eyes and ears just like me. Didn't she know the ice cream man was just outside?

Aunt Baby Doll: We have ice cream in the freezer. You can have some after dinner.

Me: (Whining) Nooooooo. It's not the same.

Aunt Baby Doll: No. You don't need that junk.

Me: Why not? Everybody else is having it.

Aunt Baby Doll: I said no. Now go back outside and stop pestering me.

When I head back outside empty-handed, I'm more crushed than the ice in a snow cone. Everybody has ice cream but me. The other kids look at me with pity. I look at their ice cream with longing and envy. All I wanted was an ice cream treat like everybody else had.

My ice cream cravings only became more intense. There's nothing like wanting something that you've been told, for some inexplicable reason, you can't have.

A Joyous Outing

My aunt must have picked up on my discontent because that evening after dinner she announced that we're going for a ride. She didn't say where we were going. Nor do I remember asking. All I remember is that we piled into her cream-colored Chevrolet, and off we went.

Soon we pulled into a shopping center. My aunt led me into a store, Save-On Drugs. As we got near the back of the store, my eyes lit up when I saw something I had never seen before—a cold case filled with every flavor of homemade, hand-dipped ice cream my little kid's mind could imagine. I was speechless with delight and awe as I stood in front of this huge, colorful display of luscious treats—my mind was on ice cream overload.

My mouth watered as we went through all of the flavors. I got to pick whatever flavor I wanted, one scoop on a cone. It was such a hard decision. But how could I pass up the strawberry ice cream with big chunks of frozen strawberries that were staring at me?

My aunt chose her favorite: black walnut. Now that I think about it, she was probably the real ice cream junky, and the trip to Save-On was really to satisfy her sweet tooth, not mine. Be that as it may, I was happy to be a beneficiary of the trip.

Savoring the Flavorful Memories

We took our ice cream back to the car where we sat, talked, and laughed until we finished every bit. I have no idea what we talked about or for how long. I just remember that it was good.

The next day when the ice cream man came through the neighborhood, I barely paid it any mind. I knew something much better, something special, was waiting for me. You might say I had been spoiled.

My love affair with ice cream had just begun.

Restraint

These days, I still love ice cream just like I did in 1962. But when the COVID-19 pandemic struck America in the spring of 2020, I gave up ice cream. There was something particularly dangerous about eating something fatty and sugary like ice cream when it was impossible to go to work out or even hit the tennis courts because everything was shut down or restricted. So, there was an extended period in 2020 that I went without ice cream, not even a single scoop. No frozen yogurt, no sherbet, no soft-serve, or hand-dipped ice cream touched my lips. Not one big bowl of Blue Bell (remember, I am from the South), not a scoop of Pitango Gelato, not a pint of Ben and Jerry's, Häagen-Dazs or Halo, which I love, entered my mouth. I can't even remember the last time I ate a half-gallon of creamy, delicious double chocolate ice cream. You read that right; I said a half-gallon!

Even though I chose not to eat ice cream during the pandemic, I know the time will come when ice cream and I are reunited. Quite honestly, I just can't imagine living in a world without ice cream.

It's Not About the Food

It's About the Story Behind the Food

And I Would Love to Learn More About Your Food Story

FOOD STORY #16: CRÈME DE LA CRÈME

Soon, whenever I heard the familiar sing-song sound of the soon-to-be-arriving ice cream truck, it didn't even phase me.

"When I head back outside empty-handed, I'm more crushed than the ice in a snow cone. Everybody has ice cream but me. The other kids look at me with pity. I look at their ice cream with longing and envy. All I wanted was an ice cream treat like everybody else had."

Does ice cream really make everything better?

Please share another ice cream Food Story with me here: michellep@leavinglarge.com

FOOD STORY 17

Road Trippin'

ROAD TRIPPIN'

The first road trip that I remember was a nearly 1,600-mile ride from Marshall, Texas to Compton, California, in the summer of 1961. My Aunt Baby Doll and her husband Daddy Al had come to pick me and, one of my favorite cousins, Bernard up on the way back from Mississippi so we could spend the summer in California.

Before dawn we hit the road in their 1950s Pontiac so we could "make good time." There will be "no unnecessary stops," we were warned. "Hit the bathroom before we leave because we're not stopping. We're going straight through." Of course, it's not possible to drive 1600 miles "straight through." But the overall idea was to minimize the need to stop for this and that. It was, after all, 1961 and because of segregation and Jim Crow, Blacks were not welcome in many places on America's burgeoning highways.

To help avoid having to stop for food, my Aunt Baby Doll put a big red and white cooler in the backseat. It was filled with ice, snacks, sodas, and fried chicken that my grandmother had made the night before at Daddy Al's request.

California Dreaming

Bernard and I were wedged in between the bags, suitcases, boxes, and cooler. Since there would not be any stops on this 1600-mile journey—except for my aunt and uncle to take turns at the wheel so each of them could get some sleep—we also had pillows and my special lavender blanket. My cousin and I played games to keep ourselves busy. Bernard taught me how to signal to the truckers to get them to honk their big horns whenever we passed them. It was such fun.

A huge dust storm engulfed the car somewhere in west Texas or New Mexico. By the time it was over, reddish-brown dust covered the entire car and every surface of the interior even though the windows were rolled up.

My uncle would speed whenever he thought he could, and the dust made it less dangerous to do so. From time to time the heat and humming of the car as it cruised down the highway would eventually lull us to sleep.

I didn't know exactly what or where California was, but I knew we were headed there, and it was going to be special.

Stopping at Stuckey's

Most times, whenever we stopped, it was to get gas or take a bathroom break. But there was one place where we finally got to go inside. It was called Stuckey's.

I didn't know it at the time, but Stuckey's was one of the few convenience stores in the South that didn't discriminate against Black people. Which explains why—beyond the fact that we had eaten all the food in the cooler—it was the first place where we got to go inside.

In case anyone doubts that, consider what Ethel "Stephanie" Stuckey, the granddaughter of the founder of W.S. Stuckey's chain had to say in April of 2020 when she was asked if there were any secrets about Stuckey's that she wished more people knew.

Stephanie said, "One of the many aspects of Stuckey's history that makes me proud is the way my grandfather handled race relations during the Jim Crow era in the deep South. From time to time, I've been approached by African Americans in their 60s and 70s who thanked me for my grandfather's compassion towards them and his fight to ensure the stores were open to all visitors."

Now that I'm in my 60s myself, you can add my name to the list of African Americans who are thankful that Stuckey's was fully open to all regardless of the color of our skin.

Pecan Logs and Souvenirs

For us kids, being in Stuckey's was like being, well, a kid in a candy store. We were both wide-eyed in wonderment and fascinated by the endless shelves of pecan logs and rows upon rows of trinkets, toys and souvenirs, everything from rubber alligators to those Davy Crockett style hats made from raccoon hides. We were mesmerized. Still, we both knew to point but not touch. We also knew not to ask if we could have anything.

The time to leave Stuckeyland came far too soon. Sadly, and reluctantly, we returned to the car. Fortunately, the Stuckey's fun was far from over. My aunt produced a big container of fried chicken she had bought inside Stuckey's. Joy erupted as we feasted our eyes on the big golden pieces of chicken, fries, and red soda. This might have been the very first fried chicken that I ever had outside of my grandmother's, and it was some kinda good!

Our obsession with the toys and pecan logs quickly faded as we argued over who would get the biggest chicken leg and most fries.

Stuck on Stuckey's

Many kids who grew up during the 1960s and 70s would lose their mind whenever they saw the bright red and yellow sign for McDonald's, the world-famous hamburger chain that got its start in 1955. Not me. I had that kind of reaction whenever I saw the bright red and yellow sign for Stuckey's, which had erected thousands of red and yellow billboards on the sides of highways "long before the advent of McDonald's."

It didn't matter if we needed gas or not, whether I needed a bathroom break or not, or whether I was hungry. Whenever I saw a Stuckey's sign, I wanted to go to Stuckey's to relive the pleasure wrapped up in that first experience. It was never ever about food or hunger; it was about the experience which became one with the food.

Very wisely my grandparents nipped those excited requests in the bud. No matter how much I wanted to experience that original rush, that original excitement, my "let's stop at Stuckey's" was always met with cooler, wiser heads. Besides, my grandparents, who were farmers, could always say, "We have food at home." And it would always be true.

My desire to relive the joy of Stuckey's did not fade right away. Once I learned to drive, earned my own money, and bought a car, whenever I saw

Stuckey's, I would stop and buy whatever I wanted. It was like being a kid in a candy store all over again.

Reliving the Fun

Eventually, Stuckey's became a thing of the past, largely because the chain dwindled in the 1970s. But I did happen to end up in a Stuckey's at the end of the summer of 2020, during an annual road trip from Washington, D.C. to Hilton Head Island in South Carolina with my sweetie. As we stopped to get gas, all the memories of that first road trip came flooding back. I let the nostalgia settle over me as I remembered my cousin, who had long since passed away, the fun we had on that road trip and our very first visit to Stuckey's.

But the yearnings of my youth have since calmed. I didn't feel the urge to stock up on pecan logs, red soda, fries, and fried chicken. And, as simple or strange as this may sound, I now enjoy the peace that comes from being free from the desire to recapture the past through food.

I can just enjoy the memory, without unconsciously trying to replicate it. So, my sweetie and I just got our gas and continued with our trip, knowing that the real adventure was the vacation that awaited us.

It's Not About the Food

It's About the Story Behind the Food

And I Would Love to Learn More About Your Food Story

FOOD STORY #17: ROAD TRIPPIN'

Often, we would stop for gas and pick up special treats for
the ride. This was one of the best parts of the trip.

"Fortunately, the Stuckey's fun was far from over. My aunt produced
a big container of fried chicken she had bought inside Stuckey's. Joy
erupted as we feasted our eyes on the big golden pieces of chicken, fries,
and red soda. This might have been the very first fried chicken that I
ever had outside of my grandmother's, and it was some kinda good!"

Do you find that food tastes better on vacation?

Does this road trip remind you of a vacation Food Story that you would
like to share?
michellep@leavinglarge.com

FOOD STORY 18

No Daddy's Girl

NO DADDY'S GIRL

Years ago, a good girlfriend and I decided to meet for breakfast. As we pondered our choices—Silver Diner, Denny's, IHOP or someplace a little fancier—she said quietly in her naturally soft-spoken way, "I don't really care where we go as long as I can have pancakes. I like having pancakes on Saturday morning."

That was fine with me, since I loved pancakes, too. Yet, I was curious about her insistence. So, I threw her a quizzical look. She went on to explain that when she was a little girl her father would always take her to have pancakes on Saturday mornings.

"I like to go have pancakes on Saturdays because it reminds me of my father," she said. I had mixed feelings about her recollection. On the one hand, I felt warm and happy that she had this sweet remembrance of her father. But I also felt a certain emptiness because I have no such memories of my father. That's because I never met the man, let alone had pancakes with him.

For years I lived with the belief that my father did not care about me or my mother. Growing up, I spent countless hours looking through my mother's old black and white photographs hoping to magically recognize my father's face, which I was sure would be handsome.

I know he was in the Air Force because the occupation box next to "father" on my first birth certificate says "Airman." I know he was twenty-five years old when I was born, at least that's what it says on my birth certificate. My grandmother told me he was from Arkansas. I also assume he must have been special for my mother to risk her reputation and livelihood as a schoolteacher to be with him.

He was stunned by the news of my impending arrival and was ill-prepared to step up. At least that's what my mother told me. I sometimes wonder if he was afraid, confused, and needed a little time to figure things out. I know he was honorable and wanted to do the right thing by my mother and me because my grandmother told me that he came looking for my mother and me. He must have felt so frustrated, powerless, and defeated when my grandmother turned him away, refusing to tell him where we were and daring anyone else in the family to speak up. As far as my grandmother was concerned, he had broken her baby girl's heart and turned her life upside down. I believe that Troy L. Gibson, or Gipson—I've forgotten the correct spelling of his name—wanted to do the right thing. I choose to believe he did the best he could, but it was not to be. I often wonder what I might have called him, my handsome (don't all little girls think that about their fathers?) airman of a father. Probably it would have simply been "Daddy."

Three Daddies

It's not that I didn't have any father figures in my life. In fact, I remember announcing proudly to my playmates as a kid "I have three daddies." My aunt, who was listening and watching through the window, came out and admonished me for talking too much. She knew the truth. I had no daddies. I think it was with that scolding, I started to feel small, voiceless, damaged, and disconnected. I wasn't abandoned, but I felt that way. I have learned over the years that your feelings can't always be trusted. They don't always represent the truth of a situation. I grew up in a family that showered me with love. I was happy, but it was a happiness singed with irrepressible and irreparable sadness that my three "daddies" either didn't know about or had actually caused.

Daddy Petties

I had a Daddy Petties. That would be my grandfather, the man who called me "gal." I didn't discover this until well after his death, but he used to brag about me to his fellow rail workers on the tracks. He and my grandmother stepped up and legally adopted me when I was six years old. He was the one who helped me with third grade multiplication and division while cursing "this new math." He protected me from high school boys with big afros, deep voices, and slow-growing beards and mustaches. He was also the one who sat in his truck for hours, never moving, while I took my SAT for college. Daddy

Petties was the man who impatiently taught me how to drive a stick shift, and bought my first two cars—Buicks, a 1970 Skylark and a 1972 Apollo. He would, on a whim, read random volumes of my begged-for-but-rarely-used World Book Encyclopedias. "Somebody's got to read them," he would say. He never attended any of my school activities, but faithfully and dependably picked me up on time after every one of them. When my grandmother passed, it was my grandfather who paid my airfare to attend her funeral because I was so broke. I didn't fully appreciate my grandfather in my youth, nor did I really understand the impact of his presence until it was too late for me to tell him.

Daddy Paul

I had a Daddy Paul. That would be my mother's husband. I remember being told to call him that, but I don't remember ever directly addressing him that way. Daddy Paul. I tried it out privately and sometimes in the mirror, but it always felt a little awkward and unnatural on my tongue. I think Stephanie, my sister-n-law, nailed it when she dubbed him Big Paul. He was father to my sister and two brothers. When I was a teenager, my mother told me that early on he had wanted me to be a part of their family. But my grandmother had other ideas. So, it was confusing to think of this man as my stepfather. He was married to my mother, a mother from afar, who was also legally my sister since my grandparents had adopted me. Yes, it was perplexing. So, I guess that made him kind of a stepfather, but in name only. I was quite pleasantly surprised as we sat at my brother's kitchen table one Christmas morning when Big Paul, in his rather distinctive Rochester, New York, accent announced, "You have feet like your mother." I'm not sure how he intended it, but I took it as a compliment. What I'm saying is this, I'm grateful that our relationship was friendly and cordial.

Daddy Al

I had a Daddy Al, which was short for Alphonso. He died of a heart attack in 2001. His nickname for me was Pasquale, his version of "pesky," because I was always asking questions. But I'm repulsed by the mere thought of him. He was my mother's sister's husband, technically an uncle, before my grandparents adopted me, or brother-in-law post-adoption. A disabled WWII veteran, he worked nights at the post office and watched me during the day while my aunt worked teaching special needs children.

In later years, I learned that my aunt paid this man to take care of me, to make sure I had breakfast, a mid-morning snack, lunch, afternoon nap, and an afternoon snack. I sat at the kitchen table and drew while he prepared dinner for us, and I happily tagged along during his daily errands to the store or auto supply shop. He always bought popcorn for me when we went to the mall and took me with him when he visited the lady across the street. He watched me as I innocently played in the backyard, baking mud pies in the special oven my aunt fashioned just for me, using discarded grocery store boxes.

Stolen Childhood

The thought sickens me. She paid him. My aunt who-loved-me-like-she-birthed-me, who visited me daily while I was in the incubator because I was born two months premature, who took ferocious precautions to shield me from harm, unwittingly entrusted me to a monster. She unknowingly left me with an afternoon tormentor, who ordered me into the house, into bed and under the covers with him before I was old enough to articulate or explain his actions in any meaningful way. Almost immediately a sense of my own wrongness started to form inside me, wrongness that grew like a malignant tumor.

In later years, I wondered if this wrongness is what made my real daddy abandon his search for me. My innate sense of well-being disappeared as if by sinister magic, vanquished in mere minutes by this child abuser, this pedophile. And statistics tell me I am not alone.

Even now, when I am out and I see a little girl, seemingly happy and well adjusted, skipping along holding her daddy's hand, I see my four-year-old self and wonder, "Is it happening to her?" Will she spend years trying to fill a cavernous hole in her soul with food like I did? Will food become a salve for her wounded spirit and the pieces that don't quite come together? It was decades before I could reveal or reconcile the depths of my shame and despair to my aunt or anyone. Here is what I know for sure: good daddies keep you safe. They protect you. They make everything right when everything is wrong. They take you for pancakes on Saturday morning.

Unlike my friends, who speak fondly of their daddies, I don't have memories of my daddy teaching me how to ride a bike or tie my shoelaces, throwing me up in the air and catching me, twirling me around, carrying me on his shoulders, going to baseball games, scuba diving in the islands or even playing Spades. I never did any of these things with my daddy. No, I don't have any such memories to soothe the ache of my darkest hours. I am, however, comforted by the fact that he tried. My daddy tried. Occasionally, when I pass a Silver Diner, International House of Pancakes, or Denny's on a Saturday morning, I must admit that I get a little sad because I don't have my own breakfast-with-my-daddy story. Yet, I am glad that my friend has hers and shared it with me. I smile and let the warmth of her experience wash over me.

It's Not About the Food

It's About the Story Behind the Food

And I Would Love to Learn More About Your Food Story

FOOD STORY #18: NO DADDY'S GIRL

The daughter-daddy connection is far from simple.
It's complex, complicated, and layered.

"On one hand, I felt warm and happy that she had this sweet
remembrance of her father. But I also felt a certain emptiness
because I have no such memories of my father. That's because
I never met the man, let alone had pancakes with him."

What happens when the adoration a daughter feels for her
dad is intertwined with their special food rituals?

Do you have a Food Story that is rooted in
your relationship with your father?
michellep@leavinglarge.com

FOOD STORY 19

The Pastor Needs a Plate

THE PASTOR NEEDS A PLATE

I t was the first full day of our annual family vacation on Hilton Head Island—a 69-square mile piece of land that sits in the low-country region of South Carolina. After a long drive from Washington, D.C. the day before, I was looking forward to a recuperative, lazy Sunday morning of sleeping in and lounging poolside, luxuriating in nothingness, and not even pretending to read a book. That was my plan.

Then my sister—much too cheerfully for my taste—announced that she was headed to church. In doing so, she cast a look at me that was equal parts invitation, expectation, and indictment. I really tried to ignore her, but she persisted. "Oh, I look forward to visiting this church every year," she beamed. "The people are so warm and welcoming. The pastor is anointed. It's one of the oldest Black churches on the island. And they are celebrating their 150th year church anniversary." That was 2019.

My sister's sunny attitude—annoying as it was—won me over. She had enough conviction for both of us. The next thing I knew, I was dressed and buckled-up in the passenger seat of her champagne 2015 Honda, headed to church. I have no idea how that happened. One minute I was cozying under the blankets; the next minute we were pulling up onto the jam-packed parking lot of First African Baptist Church where Reverend Alvin L. Petty was the pastor. My sister, a visitor herself, was delighted to have her own visitor in tow. Me? Well, I was happy that she was happy.

A Special Sunday

It was immediately evident that this was no ordinary Sunday. Even though this was my first time inside this church, something told me that the ladies' hats were bigger, and the suits were brighter on this Sunday. As people say, they were dressed to the nines. The usher board was stepping especially high. The deacons and deaconesses were even more distinguished. Everyone was dressed in full celebration mode. The pastor and all pulpit participants were adorned in full regalia. Bits and pieces of the sermon stood out: Saving souls. Christ our redeemer. The healing power of prayer. There were a lot of hallelujahs, amens, and affirmations! And "He made a way out of no way" testimonies, hand clapping, choir rocking, and side-to-side swaying of a congregation bursting with joy and gratefulness. In the twinkling of an eye, I traveled back to my childhood and the many Sundays I spent at Galilee Baptist Church in Marshall, Texas, where my grandfather, a trustee, held the distinct honor of tossing the pastor out of the pulpit after an unforgivable transgression. But I digress. Three long hours later, after the offerings had been collected, altar call, opening of the doors of the church, and benediction, everyone descended to the fellowship hall to continue the celebration.

As we entered the lower sanctuary, we were greeted by the sights, sounds, and aromas that are the hallmark of every Black church feast, including a scurrying, but somehow precise, army of the fine and gracious members of the kitchen ministry. You know, the ladies of the church who are a queenly blend of grandmother, restaurant hostess, cafeteria lady and college dean.

Preparing a Meal

While the rest of us were upstairs immersed in the word, these apron-wearing worker-bees were busy, neatly setting up row after row of dining hall tables, adjusting plastic tablecloths, lining up chairs and arranging centerpieces. Then they took their places, dutifully "manning" their assigned positions behind the long tables of steaming chafing dishes filled with homemade goodness, serving spoons in their hands, and ready to serve the hungry souls that awaited.

The food was blessed. With plates in hand, we all stood patiently in line waiting our turns. There was plenty of laughing and hugging, everyone thankful and grateful for God's grace. There was fried and baked chicken, macaroni and cheese, fresh collards, potato salad, and iron skillet cornbread topped with melted butter. Wait, there's more. There were sweet potato pies, red velvet cakes and pound cakes, the true signature of a highly skilled baker. The line couldn't move fast enough.

My eyes connected with the serving trays. I could finally see the goodness that I had inhaled for the last ten minutes. My mouth began to water. And then, these words pierced the air, "Here comes the pastor!" The energy shifted immediately. Somebody else followed with, "We have to get the pastor's plate ready!"

"The pastor needs his plate!" sang a chorus of voices. The members of the kitchen ministry kicked into high gear. If you didn't already know, you knew then that feeding the one who feeds us spiritually is a high priority. The serving line came to a halt. I was mesmerized by the rustling, bustling, and hustling as the pastor's plate passed from station to station, loaded with extra helpings of everything. And I do mean everything—fried and baked chicken, iron skillet cornbread, macaroni and cheese, fresh collards, potato salad, sweet potato pie, pound cake, and red velvet cake.

I watched the scene unfolding before me with a dawning awareness and crystal-clear clarity: "These people really love their pastor!" And this food was a demonstration of their love for him. Their hearts, like his plate, overflowed with love and respect for him. They were grateful and appreciative of his service and that hefty plate was their way of making sure he knew it.

As I sit reminiscing about that moment, I pray the pastor didn't eat all of that food in one sitting. I spent decades in confusion, just like that congregation and so many others, consuming massive amounts of food because it was prepared and presented with love. Then I woke up and learned to make the distinction between food and my feelings. That's when, my friend, the scale finally started to move in a downward direction.

It's Not About the Food

It's About the Story Behind the Food

And I Would Love to Learn More About Your Food Story

FOOD STORY #19: THE PASTOR NEEDS A PLATE

Congregations everywhere make it their business to pull out all the stops when it's time to celebrate important church milestones.

"I watched the scene unfolding before me with a dawning awareness and crystal-clear clarity: "These people really love their pastor!" And this food was a demonstration of their love for him. Their hearts, like his plate, overflowed with love and respect for him. They were grateful and appreciative of his service and that hefty plate was their way of making sure he knew it."

What happens when food is your love language?

Can you share a Food Story that describes a time
when you cooked or ate out of gratitude?
michellep@leavinglarge.com

FOOD STORY 20

A Man at Home

A MAN AT HOME

As a result of this journey, I have lost 60 pounds and kept it off. The top questions are always, "What's your secret? How did you do it?" While there are many "secrets," here is a big one: I got a man. But not just any man.

I got a man who makes life easier and better, who makes me better. I got a man with a big and generous heart, a sweet and selfless spirit. I got a man who calmly and quietly stands strong and tall, who stands his ground. I got a man who is always good to me, even when I'm thoughtless and careless. I got a man who, for months, insisted that I drive his car while he walked and took the Metro to work. I got a man who never lets me carry anything heavy, who is always fifteen minutes early, but never reminds me that I am fifteen minutes late. I got a man who bought a big, beautiful shower bonnet for me when he saw me in the shower wearing a plastic grocery bag on my head. I got a man who will take me to the theatre and have a good time, even when he really wants to stay home and watch reruns of NCIS. I got a man who opens doors for me, walks curbside, and likes to hold hands whenever we are out and about. I got a man who ignores then loves my evil Gemini side. I got a man who knows the way to my heart is through my stomach; yet knows he must feed my spirit and soul. I met a man who said, "If you want to lose weight, that's cool. I will support you but do it for yourself. Don't think you have to do it for me."

Ironically, it was the recession of 2008 that ignited this leg of my journey to a better body and to love. For years, some might say, I was living a good life. My career and finances were in good shape. Other than stabilizing the romantic side of my life, getting a handle on my weight was my only issue. I knew how to lose unwanted weight; I had done so many times. I, however, couldn't keep it off. And then in September 2008, I found myself out of a job. Soon, I was out of savings, a car, resources, luck, and standing on the outside of my life watching it dissolve right before my eyes. My home was in foreclosure. Investment property, investments, IRA all gone, just like my self-esteem, self-worth, self-respect, and self-confidence. There were times I just wanted to close my eyes and not open them. I prayed for relief.

Weary or not, I had to go on. Losing my car forced me to walk every day. Because of my extremely limited budget, I started cooking at home paying strict attention to portions and eliminating alcohol purchases. I lost weight. My clothes got looser. Walking daily provided regular exercise, but it also gave me much needed time with my thoughts. Although every other area of my life was still in crisis and chaos, I decided to pick this one area of my life, my weight, and work on that with a single-minded, laser focus. I dusted off one of the many workout books in my library and I started with fifteen minutes a day, every day. After a few months, I could see and feel my body changing. I wanted to exercise more, but I was hindered by the size of my breasts—triple D's, maybe G, H or I cup. I don't know if I ever wore a properly fitting bra. Desperate for a dramatic change in this area of my life, I decided to have surgery. No, not gastric bypass, but breast reduction and a tummy tuck; my insurance covered the former but not the latter. In many ways, I was reborn in July 2013. Those procedures gave me a new life. Sure, I continued to walk and change my eating habits, but the surgery gave me a much-needed boost, and a glimpse of a body that I could possibly love someday. Much more than my body was transformed. Armed with this new confidence, I once again entered the dating arena. I did what people do nowadays, I turned to online dating.

I met him in October 2013, as I was looking to navigate the chaos in my life. I needed to transition out of a long-term romance while I still felt good about it. A profile on Black People Meet seemed to be the easiest, most efficient, expedient, and effective way to do it. This was not, by any means, my first online dating rodeo. Online dating taught me one important lesson: keep my expectations low. I had seen his picture and he had seen mine. His profile was short and to the point. Late 50's. Divorced. Grown Children. Single. One-woman man. Ready for something new. Ok, but profiles and pictures never tell the whole story. We traded a few emails. Our phone conversations were pleasant enough and I was feeling rather good about the meetup. "Keep the bar low," I reminded myself. That's the secret to online dating success. We agreed he would pick me up at one o'clock from my office at Morgan State University radio station, WEAA. While I was no stranger to online dating, I knew this thing could go in any direction. For some unknown reason, I didn't follow the cardinal rule of online dating: meet for coffee at Starbucks first.

"Dang, I think that's him," I glanced out of the third-floor window of my office. I saw an unfamiliar wine-colored Jaguar slowly and cautiously cruising through the parking lot. It was 12:45 pm and I was not ready. He got extra points for promptness and punctuality, although they do have their pros and cons. "It's just lunch. Don't get your hopes up too high," I reminded myself. "Well, if it isn't a good time, at least we both will have a good meal."

Over lunch I got to know Tony Williams, the man that would ultimately become my sweet sweetie, a soft-spoken, kind of shy, former chef, yes, chef, now restaurant manager for the Royal Sonesta in Baltimore.

Date #1 went well enough to inspire date #2. It turned out to be a lovely day spelunking around Eastern Market, lunch at a Greek restaurant on Capitol Hill, back to my house in Brookland, for the first of many long conversations over tea, then a quick trip to CVS to pick up a prescription for my upcoming surgery. Tony offered to drive from Baltimore, where he lived, to take me to the 5:30 a.m. procedure. I declined. He offered again. I declined again. He wisely let it go. The next day I deliberately reconsidered his offer. My knight in shining Jaguar was knocking on my door at 5:15 a.m., which means he likely left his place in Baltimore at four. Tony and I headed to Washington Hospital Center, which was only five minutes away. I was checked in, then sent to pre-op where an IV was placed in my arm. Tony sat with me. He didn't ask and I didn't tell. But I know he overheard my conversations with the nurses and doctors as they prepared me for the surgery, elective thigh lift, reduction, and liposuction, my third such body contouring procedure in four months. That was date #3.

I felt like surgery was my only option. My thighs looked like huge bulging tree trunks. My hips were too wide for my tastes. Bolstered by the recent success of the tummy tuck and breast reduction, I once again called upon the genius and expertise of Dr. Konrad Dawson. This all might seem insane considering I did not have a car, needed a new roof on my house and my front door was being held together by duct tape. However, I knew I needed a new me more than I needed a new front door, car, or roof.

Tony stayed with me until they wheeled me into the operating room. When I woke up from the anesthesia a few hours later, I felt the need to address all that he had seen and heard. I sent this text, "Everything, okay. Hope you like the new me." He texted back, "I liked the old you, so I'm sure I'll like the new you."

A few months later we moved in together.

A chef and a food addict. We had one thing in common, food. The bond was instantaneous. Many long and successful relationships are built on way less. He loved to cook good food and I loved to eat good food. We have a symbiotic relationship. When we first met, Tony prepared beautiful meals for us. He is a professionally trained, now retired, chef. Cooking is his talent and gift to the world. And now to me. We would go grocery shopping, come home, and have wonderful times in the kitchen cooking together. A typical Saturday, when he wasn't working, meant a trip to Eastern Market for fresh fruits and vegetables and a stop to taste new and different cheeses, then a trip to the wine store to load up on a variety of wines and spirits. What's a good meal without the right wine, right? Then we'd make a trip to the grocery store for the extras. We would spend an hour in Giant browsing the aisles discussing food, cooking and what I'll watch him prepare when we get home. One or two bottles of wine later, all is good with the world. Good cookin.' Good luvin.' Good Lord, this dress sure is tight!

I'm sure it's no big surprise that after a while the weight was starting to pile back on. This, after a few surgeries, exercising consistently, and really struggling to eat right. I had spent thousands of dollars, that I really didn't have, to get a body that I could be okay with. I realized later that I was eating more because I wanted to show Tony how much I appreciated him, his efforts, and his talent. The more appreciation I showed, the more he cooked. What that man can do with grilled chicken wings and roasted potato salad should be outlawed. That's just how good it was! I found myself trapped in a brutal, but delicious, cycle. I had to stop it. I had spent way too much money on surgery and way too many years yo-yoing. Besides, I just didn't want to live like that anymore. When I started my doctor's program, I didn't even tell Tony. He didn't ask and I didn't tell. I shifted my focus to pleasing myself. I started saying things like "I already ate" or "I'm not hungry" or "I'll get something later." Admittedly, I had mixed feelings. However, when I finally got clear that I needed to eat for my health, not to please the cook, that was a real game-changer.

I found my voice, defined, and set clear boundaries around food. I am no longer a child who wants to make my grandmother happy, by cleaning my plate or asking for extra helpings to show my appreciation. I broke my habit of eating to please others. I knew if I could say no to my sweetie, someone who cooks for me out of love, then I could say no to anybody.

He never gave me any reason to doubt him; in fact, from the very beginning there was every reason for confidence, and yet there I was four years into it unsure. I had heard so many stories about dieters being sabotaged by loved ones. Finally, I told Tony about my new eating habits. That's when he said, "If you want to lose weight, that's cool. I will support you but do it for yourself. Don't think you have to do it for me." He asked for my food list, reviewed it, then immediately made it his business to develop creative, inspired, and imaginative meals for me. The weight started to fall off. We have all heard that the way to a man's heart is through his stomach, right? Well, the journey to a woman's heart follows much the same path. Years earlier, Tony said to me, "Okay, I'm giving my heart to you." I was struck by the magnitude of the gift. Another person's heart is not to be taken lightly or betrayed. I realized what a responsibility it was to be entrusted with another's heart. What I didn't realize at the time was that he was also saying, "You can trust your heart with me." Interestingly, while I gave him my heart, I also turned my stomach over to him, too.

Michelle's got a man at home. A man who raises the bar. A strong, sweet man. Yes, Michelle, a sugar addict, has a sweet man at home.

It's Not About the Food

It's About the Story Behind the Food

And I Would Love to Learn More About Your Food Story

FOOD STORY #20: A MAN AT HOME

A food addict and a chef meet and fall in love.

"The more appreciation I showed, the more he cooked. What that man can do with grilled chicken wings and roasted potato salad should be outlawed. That's just how good it was! I found myself trapped in a brutal, but delicious, cycle. I had to stop it. I had spent way too much money on surgery and way too much time yo-yoing."

Is it a recipe for disaster or a date with destiny?

Please share a Food Story that tells of a time when you over-cooked or over-ate because of love.
michellep@leavinglarge.com

FOOD STORY 21

Rock Bottom

ROCK BOTTOM

L ike many people addicted to a certain white powdery substance, I've hit rock bottom a few times in my life. The worst one came in November 1991, when my younger sister Myrna and I were both living in the Washington, D.C. area.

You might think—based on the time and place—that I got caught up in the crack cocaine epidemic that ravaged the nation's capital in the 1990s. It was an era, after all, when the city was known as the "murder capital." Open-air drug markets were common, and even the city's mayor, Marion Barry, got caught for possession of cocaine in an undercover FBI and police sting.

But cocaine wasn't my problem. My dusty white powder of choice was sugar. Besides, it was, and continues to be, cheap, legal, and readily available—all the things addicts find appealing. For decades this highly addictive, white granular substance drove me to do things I never thought I'd do. Forget the other flavors: salty, sour, savory, spicy or bitter. Sweet was all I craved. I craved it so much that, much like a crack addict, I would sneak things from friends and family to feed my addiction. No, I never robbed or stole to get a fix like a crack addict might; I would sneak the sweets themselves.

Compulsion and Urges

I knew I was out of control when I allowed this bad habit of mine to encroach upon the special bond that I shared with my sister Myrna, who had moved up from Texas earlier that year so she could be closer to her job in Fairfax, Virginia. So, she was close but not as close as when we were roommates back in Texas, when we would spend Sunday afternoons lounging on the sofa watching reruns of "Wagon Train," "Rawhide" and "Gunsmoke." Who knew that watching old western movies could be so bonding?

We both lived in the Greater Washington area and saw each other as much as we could, mostly on the weekends. As the holiday season approached, we reminisced about the good old days, about how much fun we had over the years. It was during one of those times that we chose to honor the baking skills of our late mother and grandmother by establishing a new holiday tradition. We decided to make fruit cake cookies and send them out to friends and family as presents. We wanted to do something together that honored our favorite childhood "sister activity"—baking cookies.

A Family Tradition

It was only natural that our cookie of choice would be fruitcake. I come from a family of fruitcake and eggnog lovers. The holidays make it abundantly clear, there are two kinds of people in the world: those who like fruitcake and those who don't. We all loved fruitcake, especially my grandmother's. It was a confection worthy of our respect. Year after year, I watched her prepare it. This is not an undertaking for the faint of heart. The construction of a meticulously crafted fruitcake begins well in advance of its presentation, not days but weeks. A time-honored ritual.

As a child, I observed how the process would start in late September when my grandmother would gather fallen pecans from the trees that grew in our backyard. My grandfather and I knew there would be big trouble if we ate any of the pecans she was storing for the fruitcake. My grandmother would shell those pecans at night, after her day work was done. In the coming days, she would check the newspaper for coupons and sales for the best prices on premium ingredients: real butter, large brown eggs, dark brown sugar, and pure vanilla, not the imitation stuff. Then she'd remind my grandfather to pick up the whiskey she would need for the final step of soaking the cake.

Having watched my grandmother prepare fruit cakes year after year, I knew firsthand what an intense and intimidating process this was, for even the most experienced bakers. So, we settled on the cookies.

The first time we tried it in 1991, Myrna and I baked all day. It was a somewhat truncated version of my grandmother's process.

Indulgence

We made the cookies at the Capitol Hill condo I shared with my roommate, Jim. There was just one little problem: we made the cookies at a time in my life when I was seriously struggling with a sugar addiction and overeating.

A batch of fruitcake cookies exposed my weakness for all things sweet.

The cookies were beautiful—all six dozen of them. We each tasted them and agreed that they were moist and delicious. They were just the right combination of earthy, spicy, sweet, and fruity.

The plan was to store them at my place for a few days until I got the shipping containers and soak them in a little bourbon. We ate one or two more and Myrna took a few home in a baggy. My roommate, Jim, tasted one or two. The rest? Well, I ate them all–one by sweet, delicious, one. That's somewhere around 60 cookies, at 109 calories, 10 grams of sugar, and 5 grams of fat apiece. When Myrna came back a few days later to get her half of the cookies, I blamed their disappearance on my roommate. "Jim ate them," I said, lying through my teeth to cover the shame of my actions. She looked hurt, angry, and disappointed. I couldn't believe I let sugar sour our sisterhood, and all that it represented. I felt tremendous guilt; but not enough to tell Myrna the truth.

The Search for a Solution

A couple of months after the fruitcake cookie catastrophe, I found myself sitting in a jam-packed meeting of Overeaters Anonymous. I was in a low, dark place that I could no longer stomach. I had watched an episode of Oprah and learned that there was a connection between our emotions and eating. I was fascinated, to say the least. I had always felt something was seriously wrong going on with me and food. The idea that I could get a handle on this new emotional overeating thing struck a chord with me. I welcomed it.

I compulsively started searching for answers. I read book after book on emotional overeating: "When Food is Love," "Love Hunger," and "Homecoming: Reclaiming and Championing Your Inner Child" became my bibles.

These books helped me see I needed professional help. So, I started going to Overeaters Anonymous meetings twice a week and saw a psychiatrist to tackle my childhood trauma and depression. I also changed my diet—one of the many times that I would do so—and worked out twice a day.

Dealing with all the emotions that fueled my tendency to overeat was a different story. It's too much to unpack here. What I will say is this, if you are separated from your mother at birth and sexually abused as a child, it should come as no surprise that you addictively seek to escape the pain. And for many, food is their drug of choice.

Just knowing I was an emotional overeater helped. Knowing I was an addict helped. Knowing was not enough for me to get over it. It was a rocky road for sure.

Still, I struggled with overeating for years afterward—really all the way up until 2019 when I was finally able to maintain a healthy weight.

As I look back on all my struggles, it's clear I was working my way through a complicated maze of painful issues, starting in the A's: abuse, abandonment, addiction, acceptance. I can now see these issues are connected, one hiding behind or inside another, often disguised as one appears to be another.

Reconciliation and Reflections

Of all my rock bottom moments, that fruitcake cookie day gives me the most pause. A day that should have been joyful instead left me feeling empty, guilty, and ashamed—for way too many years.

It took a long time to finally confess to my sister that I was the one who ate her fruitcake cookies, not my roommate Jim. But I had to do it. It's one of the 12 steps that you take when you belong to a 12-step program such as Overeaters Anonymous. Step #5 states: "Admit to God, to ourselves, and to another human being the exact nature of our wrongs."

I'm so glad that my sister forgave me. We had a big laugh, and she was finally able to release all the resentment she harbored towards Jim. As much as I wish the cookie episode was my only rock bottom moment, it was not. There were many others before it and after it. Like when the classical radio station I was working for hosted a costume ball and I was too big to wear any of the period ball gowns they supplied. I had to find fabric and make my own dress for the occasion. Finally, all the years I spent making my own clothes in high school paid off.

Or when a few years later I purchased some candy for a client as a gift and she discovered discarded wrappers I had inadvertently left in the bag—evidence that I had taken a few pieces for myself.

Or the countless times when I looked in the mirror and saw that even with the weekly trips to the nail and hair salon, the jewelry, and whatever designer clothes I had on, I still felt defeated, powerless, and burdened by my body. None of the wrongness I felt inside was healed by my attention to the outward trappings of my appearance.

Or when I caught a disturbing glimpse of the rolls of fat across my back in a department store dressing room mirror. I stood there feeling beaten down and discouraged by bunches of discarded, ill-fitting garments.

Or the countless times I'd race to Whole Foods, Harris Teeter, or Safeway to buy a four-pack of giant bran muffins. I'd rip through the plastic and devour all four muffins while still in the parking lot, stopping only when the container lay empty on the seat beside me.

Or, when, after a massive and seemingly sudden weight gain, I caught a look of surprise, shock, and disapproval in the eyes of an ex who had not seen me in some time. Then there was that time in 1986. I was 217 pounds and diagnosed as morbidly obese for the first of many times. With the help of a top Dallas bariatric doctor who prescribed appetite suppressants, drastically cutting calories, working out seven days a week, morning, and evening, six months later, I dropped 60 pounds—hello size 14.

I moved to D.C. with the ex. A year later we split. Twelve months later I regained those 60 pounds, and then some. There I was, at rock bottom again.

It's Not About the Food

It's About the Story Behind the Food

And I Would Love to Learn More About Your Food Story

FOOD STORY #21: ROCK BOTTOM

I deserve joy and try as I might, I could not find it in food.

"You might think—based on the time and place—that I got caught up in the crack cocaine epidemic that ravaged the nation's capital in the 1990s. It was an era, after all, when the city was known as the "murder capital." Open-air drug markets were common, and even the city's mayor, Marion Barry, got caught for possession of cocaine in an undercover FBI and police sting.

But cocaine wasn't my problem. My dusty
white powder of choice was sugar."

How low is rock bottom?

You can share a Food Story about your most recent rock bottom moment here: michellep@leavinglarge.com

FOOD STORY 22

Full Circle

FULL CIRCLE

For nine months, nearly every week from September 2018 until June 2019, I visited my doctor for my regular weigh-in and assessment, a ritual I increasingly embraced. While the visits weren't always pretty, they kept me accountable. I threatened to have additional liposuction more than a few times when I grew impatient with the scale. I did not follow the program perfectly by any stretch of the imagination. I certainly ate six chicken wings when it should have been one chicken breast. As rocky as it was, it got better and easier as I stayed the course. And it happened overnight, over many nights, because adequate sleep is key to body transformation, something that I learned on this pound by purpose-filled journey. "You are doing great!" I'm finishing my weekly weigh-in and Doc is reading my body composition report. She's happy and I'm delighted myself. Why wouldn't I be? It's been more than six months since the Pizzagate incident. I can wear 95% of what's in my closet. I successfully shed 55 pounds and went from 215 to 160 pounds. I am no longer obese. At last, I am no longer a part of this troubling statistic. At 61, I am getting more smiles and looks of appreciation from men and more "Girl, I love your outfit!" remarks from women than I did at 21. I'm feeling pretty good as we sit in her office discussing my progress. Then she casually drops this bomb, "You should write a book." She said it as nonchalantly as you would say "pass the sugar-free ketchup." Let's just say I'm surprised, but not shocked. From the start, even with certain hiccups along the way—not drinking enough water, eating way too many grapes and then there was that last bread pudding encounter that we'll call the lost bread pudding weekend—she was impressed with not only my progress but the thoughtful way I approached the program. I'd achieved better results than any of her other patients in her twenty years of working in this area. Soon Doc was asking me to share my insights, inspirations, and ideas with other patients on her program, especially the new ones or those in need of encouragement.

When I would go to the office for my weigh-ins, Doc would ask me what I ate during the previous week. My answer might be something like, "citrus grilled shrimp with lemon-pepper sauce and rainbow peppers, blackened chicken with strawberry raspberry glaze and Cajun cauliflower, jerked mahi-mahi and asparagus tips, roasted kale soup." "YUM!" she'd say, adding, "Most of my patients don't have a Chef Tony and their partners often sabotage their efforts. You're lucky!" Then I would bring her a few samples. She especially liked the gazpacho. On many occasions she would say something like, "I wish more of my patients had what you have, a support system, a way to make the food appetizing and a ready-for-change mindset." My sweet, sweetie, that's what I call my partner Tony, said, "I love you for you. Don't think you have to lose weight for me, but if you are doing this for yourself, I will support you." He did and he does. "You were ready and committed to permanent change," Doc said.

As I talked about the meals Tony prepared, in support of my new way of eating, I also talked about my daily experiences and epiphanies around the who, what, where, when, why, and how of hunger and eating.

Now she'd piqued my interest. "A book?" I ask for clarification. "Yes. You should write a cookbook with the recipes, but you must also include your stories. It's your stories that make the difference for you. You really get it." In subsequent visits, she continued to water the seeds she'd planted about the book. "A cookbook? Ok. I'll think about it."

For months, I earnestly tried to write a cookbook. It should be easy enough; I thought. I worked diligently, writing daily. But it was a struggle, a burden. I was writing, but it didn't feel right. The recipes didn't seem like enough. Doc's words, "you have to include the stories" kept coming back to me. And the stories kept mixing in with the recipes and taking over. Finally, I stopped and asked myself, since people can find diet recipes everywhere online and from thousands of experts, nutritionists, and well-known chefs, what's the purpose of my writing? To share the secret of my success with others. The food was certainly part of it, but my new insight was an even bigger factor, the most important at that. I was trying to take the easy way out and just present the food solutions rather than the deeper, more meaningful stories behind the food. Then my stories came bubbling up and out, like an overflowing pot of hot grits. I was about to miss the most essential piece. "Write about what you know," that's what I've always heard. Well, I know about surviving sexual abuse, managing depression, feeling abandoned, craving acceptance, battling addiction, living in a small, southern segregated town, being a-black-girl-turned-black woman in the world, trying to make it, and missing it. I also know the heavy price of using food to mask the stress and pain of living with what I know.

I am not a trained writer. Nor am I a trained chef. I am a woman who has fundamentally changed how she manages food and the role it plays in her life. A woman who is often unrecognizable to herself, not just physically but mentally and emotionally. I am now clear that, unlike in times past, I am no longer one 500-calorie bran muffin away from sliding head, heart, and soul back down the slippery slope of eating too much of the wrong thing for the wrong reasons — 42 years of unconsciousness and bliss-less oblivion.

How did I get here? People who hadn't seen me for a long time, who were amazed by my weight loss and complete transformation, would often ask, "What's your secret?" And they didn't want to hear about another "fad diet" or workout craze. Just like me, they had been there, done that, and bought the t-shirt. "I found this special tonic. Drink it at 6 pm, 8 pm, and 10 pm. When you wake up in the morning, you'll have your dream body. It's all the rage in Europe and only costs $14.99, plus shipping and handling," is what they wanted to hear? Undoubtedly, they knew the answer was less food and more movement. But the real question was, "What made the difference this time?" The answer? It was my stories, my Food Stories. Once I shelved the idea of writing a cookbook, story after story easily flowed through me, one leading to another and then another. Each one was revealing a new food or emotional truth. I let my stories take me on a journey to a brand-new world of self-discovery and self-awareness, one that is never ending. Understanding my Food Stories—finding, facing, rewriting, and replacing old Food Stories is the secret to my transformation. The answers I found in my Food Stories have led to a better body, but more importantly they have given me the peace, power, joy, pride, confidence, and freedom that I could never find in a half gallon of butter pecan ice cream. With each story that I remembered and every pound that I lost, I better understood the truth about food: it's just nutrition and energy. Hence, the one and only problem eating will solve is the alleviation of hunger.

Food is not entertainment, joy, comfort, love, companionship, adventure, happiness, celebration, fun, protection, status, or hospitality. Overeating never offered any sustained protection from boredom, stress, sadness, anger, loneliness, confusion, frustration, heartbreak, shyness, uncertainty, shame, exhaustion, or disappointment. In fact, overeating only creates additional pain and discomfort. With each Food Story, I found answers to the questions that troubled me mere months before. Why am I here again? Why can't I get my body and habits in line with my heart? Why can't I control my weight? Why haven't I gotten a handle on this yet? Why haven't I learned? Why? Why? Why? And what am I missing? As I started peeling back the layers, the Food Stories emerged.

Here's what I discovered. In all my years of dieting, I changed what I was eating without understanding the origins of what I was feeling, thinking, and eating. Once I started to reckon with the truths in my Food Stories, things shifted seismically with each discovery. Like many, I have known for years that there is a direct connection between my emotions, my eating habits and how I manage food. Just knowing this clearly was not enough! I would lose weight, and get to a size 12, but my mind and heart were still a size 22. I put on weight because I was eating when I felt something other than hunger. And when I did eat, I routinely ate too much of the wrong things. Furthermore, when experiencing any of life's discomforts, I turned to food to feel better. Largely, I did this unconsciously. This is how our unconscious mind takes us down a road that we'd rather not travel.

It took a calorie-restricted, hormone-shot assisted diet program for me to learn that it is not about the food. It's about the story behind the food. What we eat is guided and shaped by our attitudes, beliefs, and habits around food, which emerge from our personal Food Stories, the events, experiences, and memories we have around food.

Food Stories are our eating-related experiences that create the memories that ultimately influence who we become and affect our everyday interactions with food. Our Food Identity, the way we think, act, feel, and move around food is as unique as we are individually. Sometimes we carry our Food Stories for years, unconsciously feeding and nurturing them as they grow exponentially and become more intricately connected to who we are. So much so, that the line of separation is practically invisible. Like my 70-year-old Uncle Billy who stopped eating watermelon because of a painful memory, and my girlfriend who eats pancakes on Saturday mornings because of pleasurable memories. Our Food Stories become who we are. They define us. Lead us. Sometimes for a lifetime, until we realize that our Food Stories are just that, stories—remembrances and renderings of times past. When I recognized this, I learned to extricate food from my emotions and experience of eating. I conquered my thought-life as part of my healing. That's when I got on path to create the brand-new body I desired and deserved. Identifying and separating food from feeling was a G A M E - C H A N G E R. Today, I am a woman who found liberation in her Food Stories. It's the insight and understanding I have about my own personal truths and my ability to put these memories in perspective that I have shared with you. I learned to harness the incredible power of my imagination and memory to get beyond the plate in front of me to what is important.

It's a pre-COVID Monday morning; it's a post-COVID Monday morning; in fact, it's every day of the week. I cannot decide what to wear. Every dress, skirt, suit, shirt, and pair of pants not only fit but look fabulous on me. Yes, I said it—fabulous! There was a time when I had five sizes of clothes in my closet and most of them were too tight or too small. But I still had an ounce of hope that I could conquer my weight, that I would prevail. Something deep inside wouldn't allow me to give up completely. Now, looking in a full-length mirror fills me with pride and reminds me daily of all that I have learned, overcome, and accomplished. I made peace with my body, set a goal and kept going. I faced my food demons, and didn't quit, even when I wanted to. I had the courage to start yet again. I kept the promises I made to myself—this is what I see every time I look in a full-length mirror now.

Initially, I was just tired of always being the biggest person in the room, and I wanted to wear cuter clothes. Now I can wear the cute clothes and I am rarely the biggest one in the room. I realize this journey is not about that, at all. It's so much more than looking fabulous in nice clothes. The clothes are just symbolic of how I want to show up in my own life, my career, and for the world. And now that I have lost 60 pounds, and easily keep it off, I know this journey is about finding my voice, more importantly rewriting my Food Stories daily, reconnecting daily, remembering daily.

As I wrap up this should-have-been-a-cookbook, I know my journey is not over. In fact, it begins brand new every day. Today, I'm sporting a perfectly fitted jewel-toned kelly-green knit dress with a contrasting front zipper, size 8. In the old days, the only 8s in my closet were shoes. I'm starting my day from a place of control and confidence. A quick mirror check, and I am out the door, ready for anything that comes my way. You know what? Maybe I'll write a cookbook after all.

It's Not About the Food

It's About the Story Behind the Food

And I Would Love to Learn More About Your Food Story

FOOD STORY #22: FULL CIRCLE

I know what I know.

"Today, I am a woman who has found liberation in her Food Stories. It's the insight and understanding I have about my own personal truths and my ability to put these memories in perspective that I have shared with you. I learned to harness the incredible power of my imagination and memory to get beyond the plate in front of me to what is important."

When the desire for the body that you want is
more powerful than your tastebuds.

Do you have a Food Story that you would like to share with me?
michellep@leavinglarge.com

A Note

The information in this book represents the author's personal experiences and is not intended to diagnose or treat weight loss or any other medical condition. For treatment or diagnosis of any medical condition, consult your own physician. The publisher and author are not liable for any actions or negative consequences from any treatment, actions, application, or preparation to any person reading or following the information in this book. References to any treatment modalities received by the author are for informational purposes only and does not constitute an endorsement of any kind.

Acknowledgments

I f there is one word in **Leaving Large**: The Stories of a Food Addict that resonates with you, if there is one story that soothes some unhealed remembrance, then you owe a debt of gratitude, just as I do, to a splendid army of women and men who insisted I stay the course. I call them my angel warriors. Because of them, you read in a few hours what it took me 42 years to discover. They each, in their own way, helped me breathe my truth into these pages. This book lives because of them. They surrounded, supported, encouraged, guided, listened, laughed, cried, coerced, cheered, challenged, changed, read, reread, proofed, recommended, referred, praised, prayed, pulled, questioned, bullied and, most of all, believed in the reality of this book. I am grateful to more than I could ever name, but here are a few I am heart-bound to acknowledge.

Thank you Dr. Wanda Minnis-Dyson for everything; Tony Williams for chapter 20; Wendy Campbell for feedback that hurt; Candy Miles-Crocker for envisioning what I could not; Joann Thomas for searching me out; LaDonna Gaut for providing the answer; Evelyn Anderson for your boundary-defying energy; Dr. Gary Miles for confirmation; Dr. Colleen Meyer for your magic dust; Nancy Ward for being the Atlanta link; Germaine White for being the Dallas link; Nancy Parker for eagerly reading every word of every draft; Terry Allen for being an authentic connector; Jesse Fisher for requesting the first signed copy; Nancy Oelklaus for teaching me the importance of thinking clearly; Dr. Mary Welch for bearing witnessing to the transformation; Olandan Davenport for reading my very first stories; Pat Arnold for being my mystery mentor; Jamaal Abdul-Alim for fact checking every damn thing; Pat Brown for your uncanny ability to read my thoughts; DeBora Ricks for being my double doula; Rhonda Davis for old love; Judi Bishop for embracing the stories from the start; Lynne Rivas for actively listening; Beatrice O'Halloran for making space for my creative flow; Sheila McAfee for weak side support; Mark Perdue for spot on advice; Zeke Turner for the Marshall link; Anita Williams for all that you do; Reggie Thomas for thoughtful feedback; Ben White for sharing your stuff; Dee Dee Cook Littleton for unceasing prayers; Ellis Brown for being ready to read; Judieth Welch for being the lookout; Lisa Kenner for leading the charge; Paul Perdue for being a brother like no other; Shae Roundtree for being an early adopter; Deborah Owens for pushing me out of the shadows; Ardenia Myrick for opening the first door; Leslie Hassler for on-call clarity whenever I need it; Olivia Garrett Miller for your creative genius; Christyna Giles Washington for being on the other side; Lafaya Mitchell for getting to the other side; Vanessa Collins for never letting up; Dr. Konrad Dawson for a breast reduction that's still holding up; Marita Golden for your unbelievable generosity; Tracy Chiles McGhee for being the secret sauce; Norvelle Jackson for offering your boat as a sanctuary; Lisa Reid for letting me talk it out; Leslie Davis for seeking me out, dare I say "stalking" me; Wendy Ellin for breaking out and blazing the trail; Michele Williams for expanding my vision; Veronica Brown for trusting the process; Denise Young for your quiet feedback; Kim Betton for your genuine enthusiasm; Tangie Newborn for flexibility; Carla Nelson for being my sista; Tommie Adams for capturing the Brand New me on camera; Donna Holley-Beasley for brilliant, beautiful, masterful makeup; Yanick Rice Lamb for answering my call; Marsha Jews for hooking me up; Linda Austin for reconnecting; Yvonne Malone for enduring love; Wanda Watts for being wandaful; Paul Coates for honest feedback; Lily Milner for new sisterhood; Michelle Trotter for your book club; Lisa Shannon for happy hour; Cathy Hughes for your microphone. My gratitude, like this journey, is never ending.

About the Author

L ooking at Michelle Petties today, you would never guess that she used to be morbidly obese, once tipping the scale at 260 plus pounds. After gaining and losing over 700 pounds, Michelle finally discovered that the "secret" to ending the battle between her mind, body, and hunger—her Food Stories. The personal and powerful stories in her memoir chronicle a lifetime of eating for all the wrong reasons and illustrate how events, experiences and memories inform our beliefs, attitudes, and habits around food, eating and hunger, revealing that the answers to why we eat, what we eat rest in our Food Stories.

Now, Michelle Petties is an author, speaker, Food Story Finder, experiential eating expert, and recovering food addict. Big city born, small town bred, suburban living, nowhere near retirement, still-Southern, soulful sistah who's serious about Scrabble and her morning walks—Michelle is a public media veteran who develops strategic partnerships, sponsorships, and alliances for Baltimore's NPR station, WYPR.

Michelle attended Wiley College in Marshall, Texas, as its first early admissions student in 1975 and went on to earn a Bachelor of Arts in Communications from the University of Texas at Arlington. Born in Los Angeles, raised in Marshall, Texas, she has lived in Dallas, Atlanta and Washington, DC.

When not writing, coaching, or speaking, Michelle can be found on the tennis courts, shopping for new wigs or searching consignment boutiques for deals.

Follow the Author

Instagram: www.instagram.com/iambrandnewnow
Facebook: www.facebook.com/Iambrandnewnow/
LinkedIn: www.linkedin.com/in/michelle-petties-10076aaa/page
Vocal: www.vocal.media/authors/michelle-petties
YouTube: www.youtube.com/channel/UCIbMxXOSCNH--MCNru4WuLw/
videos?view=57

Simple Requests

Provide a Testimonial

I would love to hear from you. If you would like to share how this book may have helped you, please let me know in one or more ways:

1. Write a short review on Amazon and/or wherever you purchased the book online.
2. Give the book a shoutout on Facebook, Instagram, or Twitter.
3. Email me at michellep@leavinglarge.com. I would love, love, love to hear your Food Story.

Share with Others

If you found this book helpful, please recommend or provide it as a gift to someone that might benefit from it. Spread the word to individuals, counselors, groups, bookstores, libraries, churches, organizations, and social service agencies.

Finally, reach out to me if interested in:
Finding, facing, rewriting, and replacing your Food Stories
Requesting an interview or a podcast guest appearance
Booking me to speak at an event

Much Gratitude

CPSIA information can be obtained
at www.ICGtesting.com
Printed in the USA
LVHW080837101221
705841LV00002B/242